LIFE'S LESSONS LEARNED

LIFE'S LESSONS LEARNED

Personal Reflections

DALLIN H. OAKS

DESERET
BOOK

SALT LAKE CITY, UTAH

All photos courtesy of the author.

Library of Congress Cataloging-in-Publication Data
Oaks, Dallin H., author.
  Life's lessons learned / Dallin H. Oaks.
      pages cm
  Includes bibliographical references and index.
  ISBN 978-1-60908-931-3 (hardbound : alk. paper)
    1. Oaks, Dallin H. 2. Mormons—United States—Biography. 3. Mormon Church—Apostles—Biography. 4. Christian life—Mormon authors. I. Title.
  BX8695.O25A3 2011
  289.3092—dc23
  [B]   2011032339

Printed in the United States of America
Malloy Lithographing Incorporated, Ann Arbor, MI

10   9   8   7   6   5   4   3

CONTENTS

CONTENTS

CONTENTS

Acknowledgments

In a book devoted to lessons I have learned in my life, I am privileged to acknowledge my teachers. Throughout my life my foremost teacher has been the still small voice and feelings communicated by the Spirit of the Lord. My earliest teachers were my beloved parents, Dr. Lloyd E. Oaks and Stella Harris Oaks. They were succeeded by my wife June Dixon Oaks (1933–98); my wife Kristen McMain Oaks; and our six children and their spouses: Sharmon (Jack D.) Ward, Cheri (Louis E.) Ringger, Lloyd Dixon (Natalie Mietus) Oaks, Dallin Dixon (Marleen May) Oaks, TruAnn (A. Rock) Boulter, and Jenny (Matthew D.) Baker. Other teachers include a host of men and women with whom I have served in the Church, in education, and in my activities in the legal profession.

In the production of this book, I was assisted by Elder Spencer J. Condie, a long-time friend and associate who made valuable suggestions on an earlier draft of the manuscript. My brother, Dr. (Elder) Merrill C. Oaks, and my sister, Evelyn O. H. Moody, gave unique assistance on the first five chapters, dealing with our early family experiences. My wife, Kristen M. Oaks, gave insightful suggestions on the final draft, which was then improved by the fine editorial skills of Suzanne Brady of Deseret Book Company. Finally, this book could not have been written without the essential production and research skills of my secretary, Margie McKnight.

To all of my teachers and my helpers I am profoundly grateful.

Chapter 1

INTRODUCTION

Despite resolving that I would not write another book, I felt a strong impression to write this book about lessons learned in my life's experiences that might be helpful to others. I have felt to share personal experiences that illustrate what and how I have learned principles that have shaped my life and teachings, including some things of the heart not previously shared. I do not try to treat the entire content of these subjects, so this is an autobiography of learning and application rather than a compendium of doctrine. It is, of course, a personal expression and in no way an official statement of the doctrine of The Church of Jesus Christ of Latter-day Saints.

I have always admired persons who could teach persuasively from an abundance of personal experiences, but this has been so difficult for me that I have rarely been able to do it. Now I feel I must do so. Fortunately, I have the model of other Apostles who have written books that teach from many personal experiences. Notable examples include President Thomas S. Monson's *Inspiring Experiences That Build Faith* (Deseret Book, 1994), President James E. Faust's *Stories from My Life* (Deseret Book, 2001), President Boyd K. Packer's *Memorable Stories with a Message* (Deseret Book, 2000), and Elder Robert D. Hales's *Return* (Deseret Book, 2010).

The most difficult part of writing this book has been deciding what subjects to exclude. I have omitted many key principles of the gospel that have profoundly influenced my life because I could not illustrate them with a definitive experience of how I learned them. I chose my subjects from the personal experiences recorded in my journals, correspondence, histories, and talks or from memories awakened by studying these sources. Where I have given a talk or written significantly on the same subject as one of these chapters, or where I have included text of at least a paragraph in length from an earlier writing, I have cited the source.

I hope those who read these very personal memories of my learning experiences will remember that this is an account of things I have learned, with no representation that I have always practiced this learning as I should.

Part One

TO 1971

Chapter 2

"NOT MY WILL,
BUT THINE, BE DONE"

THE YEAR 1940 MIGHT HAVE been a banner year for our family. The health and financial hardships that followed my father's 1930 graduation from medical school in Philadelphia were past. The family was happily located in Twin Falls, Idaho, where my father's medical practice (eye, ear, nose, and throat) was thriving and where he served on the high council of the Twin Falls Stake. In January 1938 he and my mother had returned from his four months of valuable postdoctoral training in ophthalmology in Vienna, Austria, and Cairo, Egypt. After years of sacrifice since their marriage in 1929, my mother could at last contemplate a life of security as the wife of a prosperous physician. In January 1940 son Merrill would be four, and in March daughter

Evelyn would be one. In August 1940 I, their eldest, would be baptized following my eighth birthday.

The anticipated happiness of 1940 was not to be. In the fall of 1939 my father was diagnosed with tuberculosis and hospitalized at a TB sanatorium in Denver, Colorado. Many of today's medications had not yet been developed, and even though he received optimal care for that day, his doctors could not stop the progress of the disease. He died there on June 10, 1940, leaving my mother struggling with a question that has troubled many faithful Latter-day Saints. During the six months of his hospitalization, my father had received many priesthood blessings containing promises of recovery. When he died, she and others struggled to reconcile his death with their faith and the numerous priesthood-declared promises of healing. Ultimately, we all learned from this experience.

Reading the letters my mother wrote during my father's last illness has reminded me of her struggles. In the first month of my father's hospitalization, she wrote him from Twin Falls, Idaho: "You shall be healed if your faith is great enough! . . . Recovery is according to our faith. . . . The blessing is ours for the faith and asking."

A week later she wrote: "If our faith is great enough there is no blessing God can withhold from us."[1]

Again and again prominent priesthood leaders, including

___

1. These letters are copied from Evelyn Oaks Moody, "The Wonder and the Anguish," chapter 9 in *Lloyd E. Oaks, MD,* edited by Amy Oaks Long (privately published, 2008), 220.

the president of the Western States Mission in Denver and a visiting member of the Quorum of the Twelve Apostles, went to my father's bedside and gave priesthood blessings that contained promises of healing. Each of these leaders rebuked the disease and commanded that my father be made whole. The blessings pronounced by others did the same. Two years earlier, as my parents were leaving for my father's additional medical studies in Europe, they sought a blessing from a member of the Quorum of the Twelve. He told them that the time would come when my father "would heal thousands." That promise had also sustained my parents during my father's illness and then added to my mother's dismay upon his death.

Finally, ten days before my father died, the doctors advised my mother, then in Denver, that they had done everything they could and that the disease would soon take her husband's life. Numb with shock, she nevertheless wrote their bishop in Twin Falls, Idaho, that "a very great peace" had come to her and that "I am also ready to say 'thy will be done.'" Her acceptance and her healing had begun, but her questions remained.

The answer was given at my father's funeral by President J. W. Richins of the Twin Falls Stake, on whose high council my father had served. This inspired leader declared:

"All was done medically and in faith . . . and in prayer that could be done for him. . . . No doubt the most earnest and sincere prayer that was ever offered was the one offered while the Master was in the Garden of Gethsemane and prayed most earnestly to His Father. 'May this cup pass by me' . . . but it closed with these remarks, 'not my will, but thine, be done.' So it was with the Savior Himself. His prayer was not answered because it was not the will of the Lord, and so our prayers have not been answered as we have asked . . . for [Lloyd's] recovery, but we have always said 'thy will be done.'"[2]

Gradually this great principle settled upon my mother's soul, healing the wounds she had felt from unfulfilled faith and promises.

Years later, in two talks given at general conference, I summarized the lessons I had learned from this experience.

In the first, I said: "Faith, no matter how strong it is, cannot produce a result contrary to the will of him whose power it is. The exercise of faith in the Lord Jesus Christ is always subject to the order of heaven, to the goodness and will and wisdom and timing of the Lord."[3]

In the second, I said: "Even the servants of the Lord, exercising His divine power in a circumstance where there is sufficient faith to be healed, cannot give a priesthood blessing that will cause a person to be healed if that healing is not the will of the Lord."[4]

---

2. Ibid., 233.

3. "Faith in the Lord Jesus Christ," *Ensign,* May 1994, 100.

4. "Healing the Sick," *Ensign,* May 2010, 50.

Neither faith nor priesthood power can invoke a blessing that is contrary to the will of the Lord.

Chapter 3

RECOVERING

I LEARNED BY UNFORGETTABLE personal experiences that no matter how far a person has fallen, there is always the possibility that with help he or she can recover and proceed forward to better things.

For me, the two years following my father's death in June 1940 were turbulent and terrible. First, I lost my father. Then, six months later, I also lost my mother for nearly a year.

In January 1941, anxious to qualify herself to earn a living for her three children, Mother left us in Utah with her parents and traveled to New York City to pursue a master's degree at Columbia University. This proved to be too soon. The loneliness resulting from this separation from her family so soon after the loss of her husband, combined with the

Stella H. Oaks and children: Dallin, Merrill, and Evelyn, 1942

rigors of graduate study, strained her beyond the breaking point. In May 1941 she suffered what was then called a nervous breakdown, which required medical supervision away from her family for many months. With faith and priesthood blessings and the loving support of her family, she was able to resume her employability and unassisted parenting in August 1942. Her spiritual and emotional strength was felt throughout the remaining thirty-seven years of her life in her leadership and service in many professional, civic, and Church positions.

Despite the tender care of loving grandparents, my third and fourth grades in school, when I was eight to ten years old, were terribly unhappy for me. I rode a school bus from the farm two miles south of Payson, Utah. The few grade schoolers on this high school bus were buffeted and bullied. I remember having no identity with these fellow travelers and being tossed about like a rag doll. Since the bus stopped at the high school, I had to walk—usually alone—about a mile further to the Peteetneet grade school. If I was late getting back to the bus after school, it was gone, and I had to walk the two more miles home.

I did not like my fourth-grade teacher, a harried older man kept on in those World War II years to teach three rows of fifth and two rows of fourth graders. My most vivid memory of that year is of passing our arithmetic papers forward to be graded publicly and of how the announced results usually put me at the bottom of the class. In a twenty-problem exercise, I usually had fifteen or sixteen wrong answers. I knew I was the dumbest boy in the room. I remember one occasion when some classmates threw snowballs at me and called me stupid.

In August 1942, Mother being much improved, our little family was ready to function unassisted, and we moved to Vernal, Utah, where Mother had obtained a teaching position at Uintah High School. There I was blessed with a stable home and family environment with the guidance of my marvelous mother. I was also blessed with a great fifth-grade teacher, Miss Pearl Schaefer, who was mature and loving. Through a wise combination of confidence and challenge, she put me back on the path of learning and gave me many happy memories.

These experiences taught me firsthand that when a person is not performing well, there are many possible reasons, some not of his own choosing. I am forever grateful for a marvelous mother and a wise and loving teacher. Their faith in me encouraged me in the thought that I could amount to something, as we said in those days.

Given love and opportunity, every child and adult can recover. All who know this and have the capacity to help others should assist as they can.

Chapter 4

TEMPLE TEACHINGS

THE MOST SIGNIFICANT ACADEMIC talks I heard during my service at Brigham Young University had one common characteristic. Instead of providing new facts or advocating a particular position, as many lectures do, the most significant talks introduced ideas that changed the listeners' ways of thinking.

The most powerful ideas that have influenced my life are those that helped me identify myself and the purpose of my life. Learned in childhood and early youth, these powerful ideas include "I am a child of a loving Heavenly Father," "I lived as a spirit before I was born on earth, and I will live again as a resurrected being after death," "my Savior, Jesus Christ, saves me from death and sin," and "our family can be together forever."

The temple and its teachings are at the center of all these powerful ideas. In a Christmas memory I wrote for the *Church News,* I described an early lesson on this subject:

"As a 12-year-old deacon, I was pleased to accompany the bishop to deliver Christmas baskets to the widows of our ward in Vernal, Utah. The backseat of his car was filled with baskets of grapefruit and oranges. This was during World War II, when grapefruit and oranges were scarce, so they were quite a treat. He waited in the car while I took a basket to each door and said, 'The bishop asked me to give you this Christmas basket from the ward.'

"When we had delivered all the baskets but one, the bishop drove me home. There he handed me the last basket and said, 'This is for your mother.' Before I could reply, he drove away. . . .

"I stood in front of our house, snowflakes falling on my face, holding the basket and wondering. We had been delivering baskets to widows, but I had never thought of my mother as a widow. I had never heard her refer to herself as a widow. I wondered why anyone would think my mother was a widow.

"That Christmas experience was formative in my understanding of the eternal family and in my appreciation for the faith of my mother. She always taught us that we had a father and she had a husband and that we would always be a family because of their temple marriage."[1]

I have been blessed with other powerful ideas about the temple. When I went for the first renewal of my temple recommend, my bishop, Chauncey C. Riddle (a professor at BYU), taught me this principle. "Everything that occurs in the temple fits into one of three categories," he said, "(1) teachings, (2) covenants, and (3) promised blessings." That wonderful teaching to a young married man was a powerful idea that permanently guided my thinking about the temple experience we call the endowment.

Many years later I read another powerful idea about the covenant parts of the temple experience. Dr. John A. Widtsoe, then a professor and later a member of the Quorum of the Twelve Apostles, spoke these words in a 1920 lecture in the Assembly Hall on Temple Square:

"Many young people object to temple work because, 'We must make covenants and promises, and we do not like to be tied; we want full freedom.' This objection arises from a misunderstanding of the meaning of covenants. Knowledge becomes serviceable only when it is used; the covenant made in the temple, or elsewhere, if of the right kind, is merely a promise to give life to knowledge by making knowledge useful and helpful in man's daily progress. Temple work, or any other work, would have no meaning

---

1. "Christmas Memory," *Church News*, December 11, 2010.

unless accompanied with covenants. It would consist simply of bits of information for ornament; the covenant gives life to truth; and makes possible the blessings that reward all those who use knowledge properly."[2]

Putting that idea with the teaching of my bishop, I learned to think of the temple ceremony in these three parts: (1) we are taught, (2) we make covenants about how we will use the knowledge and other gifts God has given us, and (3) we are promised blessings if we do so. These powerful ideas have enriched my personal life and influenced my teaching of others.

Powerful ideas, such as those taught in the temple, change our thinking and our actions.

---

2. John A. Widtsoe, "Temple Worship," *Utah Genealogical and Historical Magazine* 12 (1921): 61.

Chapter 5

THE INFLUENCE OF
FAMILY HISTORIES

I HAVE BEEN GREATLY INFLUENCED by the histories of my pioneer ancestors, feeling strongly the duty to emulate their great qualities. Here I share two examples, which illustrate the importance of obediently following the prophet and the importance of bearing children and teaching them honesty.

I.

During the two childhood years I lived with my grandparents and during the ensuing five summers I worked on their farm, my grandmother filled me with stories of her pioneer ancestors—persons she had known during her childhood in Castle Dale, Utah. When she was six and a half years old, her father, Abinadi Olsen, received a mission call from "Box B" in Salt Lake City. He was called to preach and teach in the Samoan islands, a place so unknown and far away from Castle Dale that his pioneer mother knit him pairs of heavy wool socks to wear on his mission. In January 1895, Abinadi obediently left his wife and four children, my grandmother being the eldest. During his absence of three and a half years, his faithful wife, Hannah, my grandmother's mother, labored as a school janitor, house cleaner, and dressmaker to support him and their family.

Hannah's cheerful obedience to a prophet's call was inborn. Her parents, Orange and Hanna Olsson Seely, had done the same. In 1877 they were happily established in Mount Pleasant, Utah, where Orange was serving as a bishop and where their industry had earned them what Hanna later described as the finest home in Mount Pleasant. Then President Brigham Young called for leaders to go east over the mountains to colonize what is now Emery County, at that time barren and unpromising. Obediently, Orange and a pioneering party set forth over the mountain in October 1877.[1] Two years later, Orange moved Hanna and their seven children, then ages one to sixteen, constructing their own wagon road as they struggled up the steep canyon. They spent their first year in a one-room log cabin with a

---

1. Andrew Jenson, *Encyclopedic History of the Church of Jesus Christ of Latter-day Saints* (Salt Lake City: Deseret News Publishing Company, 1941), 226–27.

Orange and Hanna Seely, about 1894

dirt floor. Many years later, toward the end of her long life, Hanna wrote:

"The first time I ever swore was when we landed here. I said, 'Damn a man that would fetch a woman to such a God-forsaken country.'"[2]

Some may wonder why I find those words so faith-promoting. They speak to me of a great-great-grandmother who did not deny her very mortal emotions but nevertheless went forward in obedience to do what she was called to do. She and her husband, who gave long and honored service in the Church, community, and state legislature, are great examples of the fruits of obedience to priesthood direction.

_____

2. Hanna Olsson Seely, single-page, handwritten personal history, no date; copy in author's possession.

II.

My father was one of sixteen children raised in poverty on a family farm near Vernal, Utah. His parents were both descended from early pioneers. His mother was faithful and spiritual. His father worked valiantly to support their large family. He had little inclination for Church activity, but he had a great sense of community responsibility, and he was a stickler for honesty.

When a cousin and I wrote our grandparents' history twenty-five years ago, we concluded with these words, which describe some family accomplishments and values that have influenced me profoundly:

"The succeeding generations have followed in the best traditions of Janett and William [Oaks]. As of January 1, 1987, their descendants (in addition to their 16 children) were 48 grandchildren, 185 great-grandchildren, and 112 great-great-grandchildren, making a total of 361 descendants. . . . William and Janett can hardly have dreamed of such a posterity when they began their married life 96 years earlier. Viewing their family from an eternal perspective, these descendants can see that the faith and freedom and prosperity that blesses their lives is rooted in the struggles, trials, and triumphs of the ancestors recorded in this book."[3]

3. Linda M. Dursteler and Dallin H. Oaks, *The William Hyrum Oaks and Janett Bethers Family* (privately published, 1987), 187–88.

We concluded by quoting this summary written decades earlier by their eldest son (our uncle), Dr. L. Weston Oaks:

"Rearing their family of fourteen children [two more had died in childhood] was the greatest achievement of William and Janett Oaks, and the one of which they were most proud. Neither of them had any particular longing for material wealth except as it would aid them in this life's work of parental responsibility. In their eyes it was far more important that each of their children grow up to be noted for honesty and integrity than that any one of them should make a mark in the world. Both worked unceasingly all the days of their lives and taught their children to love work."[4]

When individuals and families search out their ancestors' inspiring actions and words, they will receive strength and direction for their own lives.

---

4. Ibid., 188.

Chapter 6

HONOR THE SABBATH DAY

FOR ME, THE PRINCIPLE OF not doing school work on the Sabbath came late, but I learned it in time to qualify for its rich blessings in law school.

During high school and college I worked in a radio station that was on the air eighteen hours a day, seven days a week. I routinely worked on the Sabbath. When I left for law school—a huge new challenge in my life—my mother reminded me that in medical school in Philadelphia my father never studied on Sunday. He felt that he could do more in six days with the help of the Lord than he could do in seven days without it. He believed that by refraining from studying on the Sabbath—even in the difficult challenges of medical school—he would receive the blessings of the Lord.

That powerful parental example, communicated at just

the right time, prompted me to do the same. Study was my work, and the Lord had commanded us to labor for six days and rest on the seventh. I followed my father's example and my mother's gentle teaching, and I was also blessed for it.

My Sabbath observance led to some valuable conversations about Sabbath observances. I was in a study group with an Orthodox Jewish classmate. On a Friday afternoon he said he had to leave to catch the train so he would not be traveling when the Sabbath (Shabbat) began at sunset. I walked to the train with him, continuing our study discussions along the way. As we drew near the station, our conversation turned to the Sabbath. I expressed my admiration for his faithful observance of the Sabbath and commented that I also never studied on the Sabbath. He responded, "Oh, I study on the Sabbath, but my study is not as effective as it is on the other days because I cannot use my pencil to underline." He explained that the pencil was a tool, and he could not use a tool on the Sabbath.

I pondered the contrast between our Sabbath observances. He had a set of rules prescribing what he could not do. I was trying to follow a set of principles. I believed that I should labor hard for six days at my work, which was studying law, and should, therefore, refrain from student-like labor on the Sabbath.

Lest I seem critical of my friend's Sabbath practices, I must add that as I have learned more about observant Jews' activities on the Sabbath day, I have concluded that their practices are in several respects superior to mine and those of many other Latter-day Saints. For them the Sabbath is not so much about prohibitions as it is about remembering and worshipping God and rejoicing in His blessings to His people. The family gathers. They may attend synagogue, but otherwise Sabbath activities center on family togetherness, including parents invoking blessings on their children. A prominent rabbi has given this description:

"The Jewish family has a holy purpose beyond itself and even beyond the social realm. Its purpose is to sanctify, through living God's Word and Way, all aspects of life. . . . The family is the central institution of Jewish life around which daily, weekly and annual religious observance revolves. . . .

"Accordingly, a whole day is set aside for focus not only upon family and community, but upon the rediscovery of inner-being, the human soul and its relationship with God and with His Creation as a whole. In the traditionally observant Jewish home, the intrusions of modern entertainment and consumerism are held at bay for one full day in the week, inculcating a sense of perspective, proportion and a scale of moral values. Moreover, in many a modern home, the opportunity for family to just come together in celebration, let alone to join in religious devotion, discussion and song, has become exceptionally rare. In the traditional Jewish family, this is a weekly event—a whole day of such devotion, strengthening the family bonds and nurturing a religio-ethical value system and world outlook."[1]

The Sabbath was given as a sign between the God of Israel and His people. It came with a promise. We can qualify for promised blessings and receive help in pushing back against corrupting worldly influences by appropriate observance of the Sabbath.

"If thou turn away thy foot from the sabbath, from doing thy pleasure on my holy day; and call the sabbath a delight, the holy of the Lord, honourable; and shalt honour him, not doing thine own ways, nor finding thine own pleasure, nor speaking thine own words:

"Then shalt thou delight thyself in the Lord; and I will cause thee to ride upon the high places of the earth, and feed thee with the heritage of Jacob thy father: for the mouth of the Lord hath spoken it" (Isaiah 58:13–14).

---

1. David Rosen, "The Family in Judaism: Past, Present and Future, Fears and Hopes," 6–10, www.rabbidavidrosen.net. Rabbi Rosen served as the international director of Interreligious Affairs of the American Jewish Committee.

Chapter 7

HUMILITY

I HAVE HAD TO LEARN TWO LESSONS about humility: first, what it is, and second, how to seek it and keep it.

Humility is essentially a consciousness of one's personal inadequacies. It is therefore a catalyst for learning. It is the opposite of pride. My favorite illustration of this truth is Benjamin Franklin's journal description of his attempt to overcome his natural tendency toward pride by acquiring the virtue of humility. After considerable efforts he concluded that "there is, perhaps, no one of our natural passions so hard to subdue as *pride*." For, he continued, "even if I could conceive that I had completely overcome it, I should probably be proud of my humility."[1]

---

1. *Autobiography of Benjamin Franklin,* edited by John Bigelow (Philadelphia: J. B. Lippincott & Co., 1869), 230.

If we are meek and humble enough to receive correction and counsel, we can be guided to put our strengths in perspective and use them for the benefit of others rather than the prideful aggrandizement of self. "Be thou humble," the Lord has said, "and the Lord thy God shall lead thee by the hand, and give thee answer to thy prayers" (D&C 112:10).

As for the practice of humility as the natural offset to pride, I have had different challenges at different times of my life.

When I was a teenager, I saw things around me mostly in terms of what they meant to me personally. I thought it was all about me, to use an apt description I learned later. I viewed school events, athletics and other activities, and family and Church responsibilities mostly in terms of what they meant to me personally. I desired to be complimented. As I have read things I wrote at that time—now more than sixty years ago—I realize that I had a selfish view of myself in the world and very little humility.

Humility can be learned, and marriage and children are great teachers. Church callings are too. As a young adult, I began to see others and the world around me in terms of what I could give rather than what I could get. Selfishness receded and humility took root.

As a student and as a university teacher, I experienced the fact that the process of education—especially at the college and graduate level—impresses one with all one does not know, and that encourages humility. But the acquisition of knowledge and its certification (degrees and so on) bring recognition and feelings of self-sufficiency that soon work against the humility by which they were acquired. A powerful scripture describes the result:

"When they are learned they think they are wise, and they hearken not unto the counsel of God, for they set it aside, supposing they know of themselves, wherefore, their wisdom is foolishness and it profiteth them not" (2 Nephi 9:28).

I have been profoundly influenced by that teaching and also comforted by the next verse: "But to be learned is good if they hearken unto the counsels of God" (2 Nephi 9:29).

I have been favored to learn from the humility of many humble, well-educated Latter-day Saints. During most of my service at Brigham Young University, I was also blessed with the close association of President Spencer W. Kimball. The self-effacing demeanor and tender outreach of this remarkable man made him a great role model of humility.

Church callings, especially highly visible callings, pose new challenges to seeking and maintaining humility. In his assigned charge to the newly called members of the Quorum of the Twelve, Oliver Cowdery included this warning:

"I therefore warn you to cultivate great humility; for I know the pride of the human heart. Beware, lest the flatterers of the world lift you up; beware, lest your affections be captivated by worldly objects."[2]

Similarly, in an 1839 sermon, the Prophet Joseph Smith gave this warning to the Twelve:

"Let the Twelve and all Saints . . . be humble, and not be exalted, and beware of pride, and not seek to excel one above another, but act for each other's good, and pray for one another, and honor our brother."[3]

In my current position, my greatest stimulus to humility is seeing other General Authorities doing many things—such as giving talks in general conference or offering counsel on matters being discussed—with far greater skill and wisdom than I could do them.

Each of us has personal strengths that can detract from our humility. If we engage in self-congratulation over those strengths, we lose the protection of humility and are vulnerable to Satan's using our strengths to produce our downfall.[4] In contrast, if we are humble and teachable, hearkening to the commandments of God, the counsel of His leaders, and the promptings of His Spirit, we can be guided in how

2. Joseph Smith, *History of The Church of Jesus Christ of Latter-day Saints*, edited by B. H. Roberts, 7 vols., 2d ed. rev. (Salt Lake City: The Church of Jesus Christ of Latter-day Saints, 1932–51), 2:195.

3. *Joseph Smith*, Teachings of Presidents of the Church series (Salt Lake City: The Church of Jesus Christ of Latter-day Saints, 2007), 344.

4. For examples, see Dallin H. Oaks, "Our Strengths Can Become Our Downfall," *Ensign*, October 1994, 11–19.

to use our spiritual gifts, our accomplishments, and all our other strengths for righteousness.

We must be watchful to prevent pride in our educational accomplishments, our professional or Church positions, or other personal strengths from weakening the humility we need to continue learning and progressing.

Chapter 8

THE CHALLENGE OF
INDIFFERENCE

WHAT AND WHEN I LEARNED about the challenge
of indifference in our time is evident in a letter I
wrote in January 1956. Then aged twenty-four, I was half-
way through my studies at The University of Chicago Law
School. My younger brother, Merrill, was soon to leave for
the Canada East Mission. What I wrote him then shows my
early awareness of a condition that persists today, more than
fifty years later:

"And now, if I may, I want to say a little about what
you will meet in the mission field. There were times when
a missionary feared for his life, and preaching was a rigor-
ous physical experience. Now those days are history, and
today the open conflict against the Church has largely disap-
peared. Indeed, we live in an era of good feeling toward the

Dallin and Merrill Oaks, 1955

Church. But therein lies the great challenge of this day. We are now in a period of conflict with indifference, in many ways a much more dangerous enemy than open hostility. One might say that we are now in a cold war with Satan, a time in which he has called off the active opposition to the gospel and substituted in its place indifference, indifference to the necessity for the one true church. You will meet that indifference in the mission field.

"But beware also of indifference among our own people. In this time of good feeling toward our church, we are not often called to its defense. We tend to become complacent and smug—to take pride alone in the esteem in which we are held by those around us. Our spiritual muscles weaken and we forget that our most priceless possession, our testimony, is neither obtained nor retained by inactivity. The indifferent among us soon lose it.

"There, then, is the real challenge today: for ourselves, to keep our testimonies—for the missionary, to overcome indifference.

"Let me give you an example of what you will meet. My Protestant friend is very warm toward our church. He thinks it is wonderful. He is willing to listen to me explain it at great length. And why not? He believes that all churches are right! Everybody is right. As for our ordinances, welfare plan, work for the dead, and so on, they are all right—unnecessary, wasted effort, but harmless, so all right. His church is by classification Christian, but they deny the divinity of Christ, and they deny His resurrection.

"He can't believe, he says, that one church could be true. There are *so* many of them. How can one church—indeed how can Christianity—be so smug as to think that they alone have the whole truth? They all must be right, he reasons, so let's be indifferent to the whole group of them. It really doesn't matter what church you belong to. We're all just one big family, and heaven is where you go when you die.

"You will meet these pseudo-Christians, these people who follow His name and deny His existence. They will not oppose you; they do not need to do so, for within their beliefs you are a well-meaning person. But their resistance to the gospel is real. The conflict with Satan goes on, but it is a cold war, where the opponent is indifferent rather than hostile.

"In such a time we have greater need than ever to draw near to the Lord. We must be diligent in His service, courageous in keeping His commandments, and receptive to the promptings of His Spirit. We must seek after and actively cultivate our testimonies, guarding always against the indifference to God which is the curse of our day."

We are living in a period of indifference toward God and religion and must therefore nurture our own testimonies and those of others.

Chapter 9

SEPARATING RESPECT, AFFECTION, AND POLICY

Early in my work as a lawyer, I learned that it was important for me to separate my respect for the position a person holds from the affection I have (or do not have) for him or her as a person and the support or lack of support I feel for his or her actions or policies. This separation has served me well in many different capacities.

When I graduated from law school, I was blessed to serve for one year as a law clerk (legal assistant) to Chief Justice Earl Warren. This man was not just the Chief Justice of the United States Supreme Court; he was the Chief Justice of the United States, presiding over one of the three branches of our government. I had immense respect for the position he held. And I had genuine affection for Earl Warren as a person. He was a great human being—true to his family,

With Chief Justice Earl Warren, 1958

loyal to his country, considerate of his fellow workers, and ever-anxious to help the disadvantaged. But I did not share some parts of his constitutional and legal philosophy, and I disagreed with many of his judicial decisions.

I did not allow my policy disagreements to interfere with my official responsibilities, which were to help my boss with his work. Nor did I allow my disagreements to impair my affectionate personal relationship with "the Chief," as his three law clerks always called him. As each of us noted our disagreements with him (and he encouraged us to express them to him), we always reminded ourselves that it was he—not we—who had been appointed by the President and confirmed by the Senate. Respect for the position always trumped our personal opinions on the cases before us.

Every lawyer has to learn to make this distinction, and it would be helpful if other persons understood it also. We do not have to agree with the actions or policies of a client, an employer, or a supervisor, and we may or may not have affection for that person. But we respect their positions, and we conform our actions accordingly. (Of course, this would not apply if we were directed to do something immoral or illegal.)

This separation of personal respect and affection from policy agreement or disagreement was imperative later when I served as a justice on the Utah Supreme Court. Although we had disagreements on our views of the law and how it should be applied in individual cases, we five justices always respected each other's positions. And we had different levels of personal affection for one another. All of those feelings had to be separated in order for us to go forward with our work.

This kind of separation needs to be made in many activities of our lives. For me, it even applies in the decisions I make on how to vote for political candidates. Sometimes I feel policy agreement with those for whom I have little affection, and sometimes I feel affection for those with whom I have little agreement. Always I try to remember that we must not have hostility toward or reject those with whom we disagree on policy or principle. Similarly, when we are the decision makers, we should remember the Prophet Joseph

Smith's counsel that "there must be decision of character, aside from sympathy."[1]

We should separate respect for a person's position from our personal affection for that person and from agreement or disagreement with his or her policies. We have much to learn, even from our adversaries, and we are under the command of the Master to love one another.

---

1. Joseph Smith, *History of The Church of Jesus Christ of Latter-day Saints*, edited by B. H. Roberts, 7 vols., 2d ed. rev. (Salt Lake City: The Church of Jesus Christ of Latter-day Saints, 1932–51), 4:570.

Chapter 10

THE LAW IS A
BLUNT INSTRUMENT

I HAVE BEEN TAUGHT AND I HAVE confirmed by personal observation and experience that laws enacted by governments are often blunt instruments that should be used for correction only when there is no other feasible alternative.

On January 30, 1969, a massive student demonstration seized the administration building of The University of Chicago and held it for fifteen days. As president of the university, Edward H. Levi received enormous pressure to call in the police to forcibly evict and prosecute the trespassers, who were vandalizing the building and paralyzing the university. Instead, he announced that the university would govern itself. He appointed a disciplinary committee of nine faculty members from different fields. I was the chairman and the only lawyer on the committee.

In one of the most strenuous periods of my life, our committee held more than 100 individual hearings that handled 150 student disciplinary cases. Our decisions ranged from no discipline through suspensions of up to six semesters to permanent expulsions. During this event, university officials did not call on the police or the courts for any assistance.

After the students were persuaded to leave the building, Levi issued this statement:

"The University has sought throughout this period . . . to exemplify the values for which it stands. . . . In a world of considerable violence, and one in which violence begets violence, it has emphasized the persuasive power of ideas. It has sought—and the unique response of faculty and students has made this possible—to handle its own affairs in a way consistent with its ideals."[1]

A few months later, in response to political pressures and high-level calls for federal prosecution of students involved in the numerous campus disorders of that year, Arthur F. Burns, counselor to President Richard M. Nixon, invited recommendations from persons experienced in such matters. I responded with the following summary of what I had learned about this subject:

"My advice is for the federal government and federal officials to stay out of this controversy. Spare us the spectacle

---

1. Quoted in Mary Ruth Yoe, "Edward Hirsch Levi," *University of Chicago Magazine,* April 2000.

of federal prosecutions of university students for campus-related activities. And don't subject universities to pressure to cut off federal aid from certain students. Don't create martyrs or force universities to create martyrs. The movement is weakening, and providing it with martyrs would only give it renewed energy. Keep your eye on the enormous number of indifferent or uncommitted students and faculty. Leave universities the latitude of action to win the struggle for their support. Let universities give student disruptors enough time and freedom for their outrageous conduct to alienate their potential supporters.

"Let the response to student disorders be local. Let universities, in cooperation with local law enforcement agencies if necessary, handle the problem. The great advantage of handling a disruption by university discipline is that by this means the university can retain the unity and support of those persons (misguided in my view, but that is beside the point) who would be alienated by any resort to outside force to quell a disturbance. And if it comes to force or outside interventions, local police or laws will be less divisive than federal laws or personnel.

" . . . By all means, stay off the campus, and don't make university administrators and faculty look like federal policemen."[2]

---

2. Letter, May 1969.

This principle—voiced by Levi's teaching and leadership—is a good principle for every person and every organization, especially those involved in teaching. We should do our own work and not ask the law or other organizations to do it for us.

As it happened, no federal legislation was enacted, Edward H. Levi spoke at my inauguration as president of Brigham Young University in 1971, and in 1975, when the country needed a trusted lawyer to help clean up the mess known as Watergate, Edward H. Levi was appointed attorney general of the United States.

Laws enacted by governments are often blunt instruments. We should do all that we can for ourselves and through private organizations before seeking to solve problems by law or other government action.

Chapter 11

TURNING POINTS
IN LIFE

T HERE ARE TIMES IN EVERY LIFE when a decision in a seemingly small matter turns out to have enormous consequences. So it was with a calling I received in the Chicago Stake in February 1961.

I was progressing rapidly as an associate in a large law firm. My increasing responsibilities required me to work three or four evenings per week, often getting back to our suburban home after 9:00 P.M. That was the circumstance in which President John K. Edmunds, himself a lawyer, called me as a stake missionary and a counselor in the stake mission presidency. He explained that this calling would require forty hours of proselyting per month, plus gospel study and other activities, in total requiring at least three to four evenings per week.

June and Dallin Oaks with daughters Sharmon and Cheri, about 1956

If I were to accept this calling, it would obviously re-quire some immediate adjustments in my work schedule. I couldn't see how I could work fewer hours and still keep up with what was required in my work. Yet, I could not say no to a calling that I felt was from the Lord, especially when it came through a leader who had wielded such a powerful influence in teaching me righteous principles. Gathering all my faith, I accepted the call.

That decision was a turning point in my life, the kind of event that Winston Churchill once described as one of those "sharp agate points, on which the ponderous balance of destiny turns."[1]

I immediately reduced the time I gave to my law firm employment, almost entirely omitting night work as I devoted that time to missionary activity. Yet, in the ensuing two years of my stake missionary service I suffered no reduction in my accomplishments or advancement in my employment. Indeed, my success in my work and my advancement in the firm seemed to accelerate rather than decline. On several occasions when I had an evening missionary appointment, I received late-afternoon work assignments that would require night work. After fervent prayer, I went to the firm library and was prompted where to look to complete my research assignment in record time and was even given words to include in the memorandum. In two years I did not have to break one missionary appointment. Feeling the Lord magnify me professionally as I sought to serve him solidified my commitment to serve the Lord first. In doing so I learned that I could do more professionally in part of my time with His help than in all of my time without it.

This altered pattern of professional work helped prepare me to receive and accept an offer in the summer of 1961 to become a professor at The University of Chicago Law

---

1. This phrase, one of my favorites, first appeared in a Churchill article titled "If Lee Had Not Won the Battle of Gettysburg," *Scribner's Magazine,* December 1930.

School. That, in turn, prepared me for my 1971 appointment as president of Brigham Young University and for all that was to come later in my life.

"Seek ye first the kingdom of God, and his righteousness; and all these things shall be added unto you" (Matthew 6:33).

Chapter 12

WORLDLY WISDOM
YIELDS TO REVELATION

ONE OF MY MOST IMPORTANT lessons on the relationship between worldly wisdom and the will of the Lord was learned in 1963, while I was beginning my service as the second counselor in the presidency of the new Chicago South Stake.

In one of our first stake presidency meetings, our stake president proposed building our new stake center in a particular city in our far-flung stake. I immediately saw four or five good reasons why the proposed location was wrong. When asked for my counsel, I opposed the proposal, giving each of those reasons. The stake president wisely proposed that each of us consider the matter prayerfully for another week and discuss it further in our next meeting. Almost perfunctorily I prayed about the subject and immediately received a strong impression that I was wrong, that I was standing in the way of the Lord's will, and that I should take my worldly wisdom and get out of the way.

Needless to say, I promptly gave my approval to the proposed location. Significantly, the importance of constructing the stake center in that location was soon evident, even to me. My reasons to the contrary turned out to be wrong, and I was soon grateful to have been restrained from relying on them.

"For my thoughts are not your thoughts, neither are your ways my ways, saith the Lord. For as the heavens are higher than the earth, so are my ways higher than your ways" (Isaiah 55:8–9).

Chapter 13

PREPARING FOR
THINGS TO COME

WE ARE ALL PREPARING for things to come. That is the purpose of mortal life, and on a smaller scale and in a shorter time frame that is the purpose of many of our mortal experiences. I have observed this fact in my own life.

Soon after beginning my service at Brigham Young University in 1971, I wrote these words for my personal history:

"From time to time in the years following my graduation from law school I remarked to June that I felt the Lord was preparing me for some special service. Often these thoughts and remarks accompanied some accomplishment or event, such as my Supreme Court clerkship, my appointment as Acting Dean of the Law School, or my experience on the disciplinary committee, where it seemed that I was granted responsibilities and realized accomplishments far beyond my natural ability. I often expressed the thought to her that where the Lord was giving me so much he would surely expect a return, and I hoped I would have the wisdom to recognize the opportunity when the call came, and the courage to accept it."[1]

That was the thought I had expressed to the BYU Board of Trustees when I met with them on May 4, 1971, just prior to the announcement of my appointment as president. Their minutes show:

"The Lord has been very good to me in everything I have done. I have received experience and callings and special favors beyond what I deserved or was prepared for at the time. When the Brethren called me in for an interview, I began to understand what the Lord had been preparing me for."

Years later, soon after my April 1984 call to the Quorum of the Twelve Apostles, I repeated the same thought in an address to the BYU student body:

"As I prayed and pondered the significance of this calling, I was also filled with gratitude that our Heavenly Father would call me to this position, where I can use my experience and spend all my time and talents for the rest of my life in his service. I have had an unusual combination of

---

1. *The First 39 Years* (privately published, 1980), 309.

professional and Church experiences. For many years I have felt a strong sense of stewardship in respect to those experiences. I have been convinced that I was being prepared for further service. Many times I prayed that when the time came, I would be able to recognize the work for which I had been prepared and be able to be an instrument in the hands of the Lord in performing it. Now, with this calling, my prayers have been answered, my course has been set for the rest of my life, and I am grateful."[2]

That is the lesson I have learned. But the principle is more important than the person. The principle of preparation applies to everyone. We are all children of a Heavenly Father who has sent us to earth with the invitation to prepare for eternal life. Every choice, every experience, every repentance and reformation, prepares us for what is to come. Remembering that important truth will guide our choices and inform our evaluation of where we have been and where we are going.

We are all preparing for things to come.

---

2. "Counsel for Students," in *Brigham Young University 1984–85 Devotional and Fireside Speeches* (Provo, Utah: Brigham Young University, 1985), 8.

Part Two

BRIGHAM YOUNG UNIVERSITY AND THE UTAH SUPREME COURT, 1971 TO 1984

Chapter 14

SCIENCE AND
RELIGION

RELIGIOUS PERSONS WHO PURSUE scientific disciplines sometimes encounter what seem to be conflicts between the respective teachings of science and religion and must work through how to handle these apparent conflicts. Others, such as I in my pursuit of business and law, can be less troubled. For me, that detachment ended when I was appointed president of Brigham Young University. This new position required me to search out, learn, and articulate answers to questions I had previously been privileged to ignore.

I began with the familiar truth that religion tells us *why* man was created; science attempts to tell us *how*. I was also helped by President J. Reuben Clark Jr.'s teaching that "the things of the natural world will not explain the things of the

With Presidents Harold B. Lee, Joseph Fielding Smith, and N. Eldon Tanner and other General Authorities at BYU president's inauguration, November 1971

spiritual world; that the things of the spiritual world cannot be understood or comprehended by the things of the natural world; that you cannot rationalize the things of the Spirit . . . because finite mind and reason cannot comprehend nor explain infinite wisdom and ultimate truth."[1]

Colleges and universities must of course teach science—facts and theories—but Church educators, like the BYU faculty, refrain from substituting science for God and

1. J. Reuben Clark Jr., "The Charted Course of the Church in Education" (address to seminary and institute leaders at Aspen Grove, Utah, Aug. 8, 1938), in James R. Clark, comp., *Messages of the First Presidency of The Church of Jesus Christ of Latter-day Saints,* 6 vols. (Salt Lake City: Bookcraft, 1965–75), 6:49; see also "Excerpts from 'The Charted Course of the Church in Education,'" *Ensign,* Sept. 2002, 58.

continue to rely on the truths of religion. In the study of science, teachers and students with religious faith have the challenge to define the relationship of science and religion in their thinking. They have the special advantage of seeing countless scientific evidences of the Divine Creator. In those exceptional circumstances where science and religion seem to conflict, they have the wisdom to wait patiently in the assurance that truth will eventually prevail. In doing so, most conclude that religion does not have the answers to all questions and that some of what science "knows" is tentative and theoretical and will be replaced in time by new discoveries and new theories.

Some try to deal with apparent conflicts by compartmentalizing science and religion—one in one category, such as Monday through Saturday, and the other in another category, such as Sunday. That was my initial approach, but I came to learn its inadequacy. We are supposed to learn by *both* reason and revelation, and that does not happen when we compartmentalize science and religion. Our searchings should be disciplined by human reason and also enlightened by divine revelation. In the end, truth has only one content and one source, and it encompasses both science and religion.

When I was president of BYU, a student wrote me to complain that we "are not using the teachings of the prophets . . . in our classrooms as we could." He cited the teaching in one particular department as having a lack of balance, criticizing the prototype of a professor who "has a Ph.D. in his academic discipline and the equivalent of an eighth-grade education in the gospel."[2] The reverse is also true: a doctorate-level knowledge of the gospel will not suffice if one is poorly prepared in his or her individual discipline.

Latter-day Saints should strive to use both science and religion to extend knowledge and to build faith. But those who do so must guard against the significant risk that efforts to end the separation between scientific scholarship and religious faith will only promote a substandard level of performance, where religion and science dilute one another instead of strengthening both.

For some, an attempt to mingle reason and faith can result in irrational scholarship or phony religion, either condition demonstrably worse than the described separation. This danger is illustrated by the case of an international scholar who was known as an expert in English law when he was in America and as an expert in American law when he was in England. Not fully distinguished in either field, he nevertheless managed to slip back and forth between the two so that his expertise was never properly subjected to qualified review in either. As a result, he provided a poor imitation in both. A

2. Letter, August 12, 1977.

genuine mingling of the insights of reason and revelation is infinitely more difficult.[3]

Latter-day Saints are encouraged to seek the truth—a "knowledge of things as they are, and as they were, and as they are to come" (D&C 93:24). Generations of our members have been taught that this Church doesn't require you "to believe anything that isn't true."[4] As President Spencer W. Kimball taught, we have real individual freedom: "Freedom from worldly ideologies and concepts unshackles man far more than he knows. It is the truth that sets men free."[5] Each of us should pursue that truth by reason and by faith. And each of us should increase our ability to communicate that truth by an inspired combination of the language of scholarship and the language of faith.

I am confident that when we progress to the point where we know all things, we will find a harmony of all truth. Until that time, it is wise for us to admit that our understanding—in religion and in science—is incomplete and that the resolution of most seeming conflicts is best postponed. In the meantime, we do the best we can to act upon our scientific knowledge, where that is required, and always

3. This paragraph is based on a talk I gave at a Ricks College preschool workshop, Rexburg, Idaho, August 28, 1991, titled "What Can I Teach My Students That Will Be of Greatest Value?"

4. Henry J. Eyring, *Mormon Scientist: The Life and Faith of Henry Eyring* (Salt Lake City: Deseret Book, 2008), 4.

5. "The Second Century of Brigham Young University," BYU Founders Day address, October 10, 1975, in *Speeches of the Year: BYU Centennial Devotional and Fireside Addresses, 1975* (Provo, Utah: Brigham Young University Press, 1976), 246.

upon our religious faith, placing our ultimate reliance for the big questions and expectations of life on the eternal truths revealed by our Creator, which transcend human reason, "for with God nothing shall be impossible" (Luke 1:37).

Each of us should pursue truth by both reason (science) and faith (religion).

Chapter 15

WHAT DO YOU WANT TO BE REMEMBERED FOR?

DURING MY FIRST FIVE YEARS as Brigham Young University president I was one of about five leaders who had weekly coordination meetings with Neal A. Maxwell, then commissioner of the Church Educational System. One day he began our meeting by asking, "What would you like to be remembered for after you are released from your present positions?" He asked each of us to write our answer on a piece of paper and consider it privately.

Pondering this inspired question taught me an important lesson. I applied it not only to my employment but also to my position as a father. I asked myself, "When your children are grown up and leave home, or when you die, what do you want them to remember about you as a father?" This question caused me to see that I was in danger

Enjoying a light moment with Commissioner Neal A. Maxwell at BYU

of being remembered for always being critical and nagging about trivial behaviors that irritated me, such as the practice of a teenage daughter who continually scattered her clothes and other possessions all around the house. I wanted to be remembered for fatherly communications of praise and love and other matters of eternal importance. Those are the communications whose memories have persuasive power.

I have often asked this question during a stake conference meeting with a stake presidency, especially a newly installed stake presidency. "When you are released, how do you want to be remembered by your stake members or by the leaders you have taught?" That question seems to focus attention on what is most important and therefore what deserves the most emphasis in Church leadership.

We should ask ourselves, "What would you like to be re-membered for when you are released from your present position?"

Chapter 16

ASSIGNING REASONS TO REVELATION

F ROM TWO IMPORTANT and highly visible events involving prophetic revelation I have learned the folly of
making additions to or attempting to assign reasons for the
Lord's revelations to His prophets.

I.

Many religious persons were shocked by the United
States Supreme Court's 1962 decision that an agency of the
state of New York could not write and prescribe a prayer
to be said at the beginning of public school classes in that
state.[1] Speaking six months later, President David O. McKay
said:

---

1. Engel v. Vitale, 370 U.S. 421 (1962).

"By making that [New York Regent's prayer] unconstitutional, the Supreme Court of the United States severs the connecting cord between the public schools of the United States and the source of divine intelligence, the Creator himself. . . .

"By law, the public schools of the United States must be non-denominational. They can have no part in securing acceptance of any one of the numerous systems of belief regarding God and the relation of mankind thereto. Now let us remember and emphasize *that restriction applies to the atheist as well as to the believer in God.*"[2]

Six months later, just after the Supreme Court's decision forbidding Bible reading in the schools,[3] President McKay said:

"Recent rulings of the Supreme Court would have all reference to a Creator eliminated from our public schools and public offices. . . .

"Evidently the Supreme Court misinterprets the true meaning of the First Amendment, and are now leading a Christian nation down the road to atheism."[4]

Decades later it is evident that President McKay had prophetic vision in warning of the pernicious effects of these two Supreme Court opinions. They *have* had the effect of

---

2. "Parental Responsibility," *Relief Society Magazine,* December 1962, 878.

3. Abington School District v. Schempp, 374 U.S. 203 (1963).

4. "President McKay Comments on Ruling," *Church News,* June 22, 1963, 2.

separating the public schools from the Creator. They *have* had the effect of "leading a Christian nation down the road to atheism." And the effects of these cases have shown the importance of President McKay's warning that the requirement that the public schools must be nondenominational, which he affirmed must apply "to the atheist as well as to the believer in God." In fact, under the influence of these decisions and their progeny, the public schools have become (1) proponents of atheism, or (2) hostile to religion, or (3) at least indifferent to religion.

What I had to learn from this key event in our nation's history is shown by a sequence of events. First, since I interpreted the school prayer decision to forbid only state-authored and state-required prayers rather than forbidding school prayers altogether, I reasoned that the case was correctly decided.

Second, when the Supreme Court forbade Bible reading a year later, I was concerned at the way the prayer-case precedent was being used. I prepared an article to express my opinion that the prayer case was correctly decided on its facts but that its precedent must be applied to avoid establishing atheism in the public schools.

Third, when he learned of my proposed article, President Henry D. Moyle took an interest in it because of its subject matter and because its author was a young law professor at the law school from which he had graduated. He wrote me that he had taken the article to President McKay, who approved its publication in the *Improvement Era,* where it appeared in December 1963.[5]

Finally, what I learned from this experience was that my worldly wisdom in writing approvingly of the school prayer case on the *facts* of the decision was just a small footnote to history compared with the vision of a prophet who saw and described the pernicious *effects* of that decision in the years to come. Exercising prophetic vision President McKay saw that the school prayer case—which I reasoned to be defensible and probably even essential as a ruling on the facts before the Court—would set in motion a chain of legal and public and educational actions that would cause religion to be separated from education and lead to the current hostility toward religion that threatens religious liberty in our society. For me that was a powerful learning experience on the folly of trying to understand prophetic vision in terms of worldly wisdom.

II.

When I went from Utah to study law in Chicago in the fall of 1954, I had my first personal encounter with the fact that persons of African ancestry could not be ordained to the priesthood. At that time and for nearly the next quarter century, this prohibition—which I and most other faithful Latter-day Saints accepted as a revelation to a succession of

---

5. "Antidotes for the School Prayer Cases," *Improvement Era,* December 1963, 1048–50, 1134–36.

prophets—was deeply troubling to many and an increasingly awkward position for the Church. Many, especially those in academic life, sought for reasons, and quite a few gospel students undertook to provide them. For a time I sought to provide reasons to help my own thinking and to strengthen fellow Latter-day Saints. Later in my Chicago years (1954–71) I saw that this attempt was fruitless. I came to realize that I should support prophetic revelation without relying on the reasons mortals gave for it.

In June 1978 we were thrilled when President Spencer W. Kimball, our prophet-president, announced that "all worthy male members of the Church may be ordained to the priesthood without regard for race or color" (Official Declaration 2). The direction was changed by revelation, and with that revelation the reasons mortals had given for the prior direction were all swept away.

In a 1988 interview on the tenth anniversary of the revelation on the priesthood, I explained my attitude toward attempts to supply mortal reasons for divine revelation:

"If you read the scriptures with this question in mind, 'Why did the Lord command this or why did he command that,' you find that in less than one in a hundred commands was any reason given. It's not the pattern of the Lord to give reasons. We [mortals] can put reasons to revelation. We can put reasons to commandments. When we do, we're on our own. Some people put reasons to the one we're talking about here, and they turned out to be spectacularly wrong. There is a lesson in that. . . . I decided a long time ago that I had faith in the command and I had no faith in the reasons that had been suggested for it."

When asked if I was even referring to reasons given by General Authorities, I replied:

"I'm referring to reasons given by general authorities and reasons elaborated upon . . . by others. The whole set of reasons seemed to me to be unnecessary risk taking. . . . Let's don't make the mistake that's been made in the past, here and in other areas, trying to put reasons to revelation. The reasons turn out to be man-made to a great extent. The revelations are what we sustain as the will of the Lord and that's where safety lies."[6]

Mortals should not attempt to provide reasons for Divine commandments or revelations.

---

6. "Apostles Talk about Reasons for Lifting Ban," *Daily Herald,* Provo, Utah, June 5, 1988, 21 (AP).

Chapter 17

ADVERSITY

WITH THE DEATH OF MY FATHER, I had an early introduction to adversity. But my understanding of the purpose of adversity came later, when I realized the importance of my mother's frequent reliance on father Lehi's teaching to a son who had suffered "afflictions and much sorrow" from the actions of his older brothers:

"Nevertheless, Jacob, my first-born in the wilderness, thou knowest the greatness of God; and he shall consecrate thine afflictions for thy gain" (2 Nephi 2:1–2).

I often heard my mother say that the Lord consecrated affliction for her gain because her husband's death compelled her to develop her talents and serve and become something that she would never have become without that seeming tragedy.

Adversity is an occasional or even a constant companion for each of us throughout our lives. We cannot avoid it. It is a reality—and indeed one of the purposes—of mortal life. What is important is how we react to it. Will our adversities bear us down, or will we go forward relying on the promise of God, who does not shield us from every adversity but who gives us the guidance and strength that makes it possible for us to endure and progress?

Some people exploit their adversities to encourage others to look on them with pity and to place them in a special category that excuses nonperformance. Others, as father Lehi taught, accept their adversities and go forward, relying on God's blessings to help them do their best.

I learned from my mother's example and the examples of others that the courageous faith and action of one person in coping with adversity can bless others who are strengthened by their example. Thousands were comforted and strengthened by the example of President Spencer W. Kimball. During his long lifetime, he was tortured by severe physical afflictions, including life-threatening heart ailments and the devastating throat cancer that crippled his voice. His stalwart response to these adversities has inspired all of us in responding to our own trials and adversities.

In a 1995 talk to Brigham Young University students later published in the *Ensign,* I shared this example of what was once thought an adversity now being recognized as a blessing:

With President Spencer W. Kimball at BYU commencement exercises, about 1975

"We may look on the shortage of money and the struggle to find rewarding employment as serious adversities. I remember such experiences and feelings, and I am unpersuaded that relative poverty and hard work are greater adversities than relative affluence and free time. . . . For many, though not all, material wealth and abundant free time are spiritual impediments.

"I am sure that the skills and discipline and soul power that result from overcoming the challenge of material shortages open the door for extraordinary blessings. I offer one small personal example. As poor graduate students in Chicago, my wife and I did not have the resources to telephone home, except for very short calls on special holidays. We had to keep in touch by long, weekly letters which each of us typed. The composition of those letters developed writing skills that have blessed each of our lives for the ensuing 40-some years. We would have been deprived of significant growth if we could have simply picked up the telephone and communicated in the almost effortless and sometimes almost thoughtless way that would have been available if we had had more money. I am an advocate of letters among loved ones, and my preference has been reinforced as I have written family histories and rejoiced in the details of loved ones' lives that have been preserved in writing rather than lost on some electronic highway."[1]

A loving Heavenly Father will consecrate our afflictions for our gain.

---

1. "Adversity," *Ensign,* July 1998, 10.

Chapter 18

FEELINGS

CONTRARY TO MY LEGAL TRAINING, I have come to realize that feelings are often more important than facts.

The law doesn't have much to do with feelings. A feeling is rarely actionable or even admissible. But our most important decisions, though accompanied by a careful study of facts, are usually most immediately motivated by feelings. Who we marry is an example. What fact or facts, unaccompanied by feelings, would motivate that decision?

Feelings are vital to the process of revelation. In a talk later published in the *New Era,* I listed eight purposes or functions of revelation. They were testifying, prophesying, comforting, uplifting, informing, restraining, confirming, and impelling.[1] Significantly, seven of these eight—all except informing—come as a feeling. For example, we should always be prepared to act upon an impression when we "feel that it is right" (D&C 9:8), even though it is not justified by the facts.

If we cultivate the sensitive spiritual receptor all have been given and are expected to use, a feeling of doubt or foreboding will warn us away from ethical or moral pitfalls. If we stray from the prescribed path, a feeling of guilt will move us to repentance. If we ignore those feelings and neglect our spiritual life to an extreme point, we suffer the result mentioned in the scripture that describes persons who were "past feeling" the "still small voice" (1 Nephi 17:45).

A personal experience illustrates how the Holy Spirit teaches us through our feelings. This experience is especially significant because it involved the feelings of a person not familiar with revelation.

A little over thirty years ago three elected deputies of the Supreme Soviet visited Salt Lake City. I took them to various locations on Temple Square and then into the Tabernacle, where they heard the Sunday morning Tabernacle Choir broadcast. A few of us then met with them in a private room and told them about the Church. In response, Konstantin Lubenchenko, the senior member of the delegation, spoke

---

1. "Revelation," *New Era*, September 1982, 44.

to us. I made these notes of his remarks as they came to us through an interpreter:

"Before I came here I thought the Mormon Church was a very conservative organization of fanatics. But after seeing the beautiful pictures and statue in your visitors' center and the beautiful setting where the choir sang and hearing the choir and organ, I have a new understanding of your church."

What interested me most was his account of what he felt:

"Since I have come to the United States, people have asked me what is my strongest impression in the United States. I can tell you now. It is the singing of your choir. I love organ music and choirs and have gone to hear them many times in my country. As the choir sang, I had a very strong *feeling*. Although I do not speak English, I *felt* with my heart that they were sincerely expressing my *feelings*. My relation with God was expressed in earthly *feelings* through their singing."[2]

Though probably unfamiliar with the things of the Spirit, this Soviet lawmaker had a *feeling* and could describe it well enough for me to realize that he had received a witness from the Spirit.

---

2. Quoted in Dallin H. Oaks, "Teaching and Learning by the Spirit," *Ensign,* March 1997, 13–14; emphasis added.

Feelings are vital to the process of revelation. We should always be prepared to act upon an impression when we "feel that it is right" (D&C 9:8).

Chapter 19

GOAL SETTING

I BELIEVE IN SETTING GOALS, especially the right kind of goals. I have learned that some goals can be an impetus for progress, but others can be little more than a source of frustration.

To be most effective in furthering our progress, goals should concern things that can be attained by our personal efforts. They should not depend upon the agency or efforts of others. This difference is important. If we pursue a goal that concerns what we can do, our commitments and standards can be constant whatever the circumstances beyond our control. In contrast, when goals depend upon the agency and action of others, the failure to attain them can only produce frustration to the one who set them.

Examples of goals depending upon the agency and

action of others include goals to marry a particular person, be married by a particular time, or be employed in or called to a particular position. Goals attainable by personal efforts include the lists we make of what we will do on a particular day or the resolutions we make for what we desire to accomplish in a new year. Even more significant goals of this kind concern our desires, which dictate our priorities and shape our choices, actions, and feelings.[1] Relying on the scriptural direction to pray to be filled with love toward our fellowmen (Moroni 7:48), my mother taught her children that when we had negative feelings toward someone, we should pray to have those feelings changed to love.

Missionaries can apply this principle to emphasize goals they can accomplish by their own efforts, such as hours worked, concepts taught, and rules kept. These goals are not dependent upon the exercise of someone else's agency, such as an investigator's decision to be baptized.

Effective goals should always be accompanied by plans to accomplish them, so goals are not something abstract or academic. Goals with plans to accomplish them will lead to momentum and success.

We should be willing to amend our goals or their timing, according to the inspiration of the Lord or the direction of His servants. Pioneer Anson Call, June's great-grandfather, demonstrated this principle of adaptability. He was a leader

---

1. See "Desire," *Ensign,* May 2011, 42–45.

in a wagon train Brigham Young organized and sent west from Council Bluffs on July 22, 1846. Their goal was to reach the Rocky Mountains that year. After they had traveled more than 130 miles, they were overtaken by a messenger directing them to return. They retraced their steps. Nearly two years later, under priesthood direction, Anson Call was finally authorized to proceed to the Salt Lake Valley in June 1848.[2]

The ultimate goal for personal effort is to put the Lord first in our lives and to keep His commandments. Attaining that goal requires personal effort and does not depend on others. It can be pursued without regard to the circumstances and is independent of what others decide or do. Faith in the Lord Jesus Christ and trust in His commandments and His will for us prepare us to deal with life's opportunities and circumstances—to take advantage of those that are received and to persist through the disappointments of those that are lost. This gives us direction and peace.

To be most effective, goals should concern things that can be attained by our personal efforts and should always be accompanied by plans to accomplish them.

2. See "Timing," in *Brigham Young University 2001–2002 Speeches* (Provo, Utah: Brigham Young University, 2002), 189.

Chapter 20

PERSONAL REVELATION

Latter-day Saints believe in personal revelation. Like many others, I have experienced it. Again and again my life has been enriched and my decisions have been guided by a loving Heavenly Father who answers our prayers for assistance. We follow in faith, but sometimes we do not realize the entire significance of His guidance until much later. I share one such experience that was essential for the immediate decision but also contained important (and unexpected) information about a future event.

I was released as president of Brigham Young University on August 1, 1980. With less than three months' notice of this release, I had not yet formulated any plans for what I would do next. Many different opportunities were presented, but the one that intrigued me most was a forthcoming

Taking the oath of office as a Utah Supreme Court Justice, January 5, 1981

vacancy on the Utah Supreme Court. Unfortunately, the annual salary of a Utah Supreme Court justice at that time was a fraction of what I would receive in any of the other alternatives I was considering. (It was even less than the offers being received by top graduates of BYU's law school, who were then my students.) In addition, even if I applied, the appointment depended on the recommendation of a judicial nominating commission and the action of the governor.

I need not rely on memory for how my decision was made. My handwritten journal of September 26, 1980, contains this important account:

"This morning June & I went to the Temple to seek inspiration on our decision. During the entire session I couldn't get my mind off the Utah Supreme Court, try as I might (and I did, continuously). In all of this consciousness of the prospect that I might do this I did not have one negative thought or apprehension. Nor have I had any in my deliberations up to this point. This is a persuasive confirmation in itself. Then, as we sat on a sofa in the last room, June and I prayed quietly by ourselves, and as I finished this thought flooded my mind, being repeated over and over: 'Go to the court and I will call you from there.' These were exactly the words that came to my mind as I pondered this question on the flight home from Washington on Sept. 17th, but I was unsure then whether I was planting the idea or receiving inspiration. Here, in the Temple, with a more forceful, identical, repetition, I had no such doubts. We have our answer. June has had confirming thoughts and expressed her willingness to make whatever sacrifices are necessary."

The immediate significance of the words *Go to the court and I will call you from there* confirmed my decision to apply for the court vacancy. It was not until I was called to the Quorum of the Twelve in April 1984, while serving on the court, that I realized the significance of the last seven words. In fact, it was not until I reread my journal as I was writing this book that I was reminded of that portion of the personal revelation. I had recorded it faithfully but without understanding its long-term significance. That frequently happens with personal revelation. It usually does not burst forth with a complete picture of the course of action one should pursue, including an understanding of all of its consequences.

Personal revelation often follows the Lord's pattern of gradual disclosure, "line upon line; here a little, and there a little" (Isaiah 28:10).

Chapter 21

LEADERSHIP

I HAVE BEEN PRIVILEGED to exercise leadership responsibilities in family and Church and in business, education, military, and charitable organizations. By watching
leaders, by experiencing their leadership, and by exercising
leadership responsibilities myself, I have learned some basic
principles that have value in each of these areas.

My interest in leadership began with my teenage reading
of the biographies of World War II military leaders. In college and law school my interest expanded to the biographies
of public leaders. Throughout my life I have observed effective (and less effective) leadership by various parents and
grandparents. As a university president I enjoyed reading the
counsel and experiences of educational leaders. Best of all,
for more than forty years I have been a close observer of the

great men and women who are leaders in The Church of Jesus Christ of Latter-day Saints. I have sought to learn how to get men and women to do an assigned job, to do it well, and to enjoy the process.

Following are seven important leadership principles I have learned from my life's experiences:

1. *Love* is the first principle. Its effect magnifies the effects of every other principle. Leaders who are loved and who love those they lead enhance the impact of their leadership and the duration of their influence.

2. Good leaders are not overly concerned with popularity, knowing that popularity follows good leadership—it does not produce it.

3. Good leaders make decisions that can be relied upon because they stick with them.

4. Good leaders are positive. Optimism is infectious. People have confidence in and work best for leaders who view adversity as a challenging opportunity and who are positively and thoughtfully confident in the assigned task and the desired outcome.

5. Good leaders are clear in defining what is expected, able to express it in simple terms, and effective in communicating with those they lead. These three qualities are so interrelated that I cannot give examples that do not, in some measure, include all of them.

President Gordon B. Hinckley was a genius at stating a principle or giving a challenge in such clear, simple terms that it drew all of us into increased understanding and more effective efforts. A few years ago he told the Church that we should raise the bar for missionary service.[1] He gave no complicated explanation. He just used that vivid metaphor to give a clear, simple challenge that expressed an ideal most of us understood and shared. The impact of that challenge has been felt by Latter-day Saint teenagers, parents, teachers, and leaders everywhere. That is leadership through simplicity, clarity, and communication.

In August 2005 President Hinckley asked every member of the Church to read the Book of Mormon again before the end of the year.[2] That simple, clear challenge has probably changed as many lives as any comparable teaching by any president of the Church within my memory. What he asked was easy to understand, and he gave a specific deadline. In doing so he directed each of us into an activity where we could benefit from the power of the scriptures and the witness of the Holy Ghost. Remarkably wise leadership!

My first lesson on the importance of a leader's communicating in clear, simple terms was by watching my Chicago stake president, John K. Edmunds. From his consistent paramount emphasis of tithing and priesthood leadership (D&C 121:34–36), I learned that if Church leaders single out a small number of key principles and emphasize them again

---

1. Gordon B. Hinckley, "Missionary Service," *First Worldwide Leadership Training Meeting* (Salt Lake City: The Church of Jesus Christ of Latter-day Saints, 2003), 17.

2. Gordon B. Hinckley, "A Testimony Vibrant and True," *Ensign*, August 2005, 6.

and again, these few fundamentals have the capacity to raise individual performance on a multitude of other subjects rarely mentioned. That kind of leadership is more effective than trying to push everything equally, like the proverbial river a mile wide and an inch deep that never achieves the concentration necessary to erode a mark on the landscape. Effective leadership requires selective concentration.

6. A good leader will be calm and unflappable under the pressure that leaders cannot escape. Such poise steadies followers, whereas a leader's panic or anxiety scatters and disables them. Sports fans see this poise in the demeanor of most successful coaches of team sports.

The need for poise or calmness applies to another kind of combat. I recall what a soldier told me about the effect of his captain's reaction to an early morning message that the enemy had broken through the lines and was rapidly approaching their position. While some soldiers panicked and began throwing things in trucks to hasten their retreat, the captain calmly sat down in a visible location and buttoned his shirt and laced up his boots. His calm was catching, the panic ceased, and the troops were ready for the orders that allowed them to maintain their position. The importance of calmness and poise is pervasive in every area of leadership.

7. Finally, no single principle of leadership is more powerful in its effect on followers than a leader's setting the right example. It pervades all the foregoing principles. President Thomas S. Monson, throughout his life and ministry, has

exemplified this principle by reaching out to rescue individuals in need and to minister to them. Like our Savior, he has gone about "doing good" (Acts 10:38). His example reaches and influences us all.[3]

Good leaders set a proper example and have love, optimism, clarity, simplicity in communication, and calmness under pressure.

---

3. See Heidi S. Swinton, *To the Rescue: The Biography of Thomas S. Monson* (Salt Lake City: Deseret Book, 2010).

Part Three

GENERAL AUTHORITY, 1984 TO PRESENT

Chapter 22

LEARNED FROM
LEGAL TRAINING

W<small>E ALL HAVE A TREASURY</small> of learning from our professions or occupations. Speaking to an audience of lawyers, I offered a general summary of the principal value of my legal training—what I took with me when I went on to a new calling. I began by telling how, after thirty years in various legal activities, I was unexpectedly called to the apostleship and almost immediately was to leave active involvement in the law.

"Suddenly I saw my work in the legal profession in a new light, as a means of preparing me for something else to follow. . . .

"Most of us will conclude our formal activity in the legal profession before we die. But the skills and ways of thinking we have acquired as lawyers will remain—for better or for worse. And when properly applied, those skills and ways will still be a source of blessing to many.

"For example, I am conscious every day that my approach to gathering facts, analyzing problems, and proposing action is a product of my legal training. So is my idea of justice. (The law has been less influential in teaching me about mercy.) If one makes proper use of opportunities, the study of law disciplines the mind and the practice of law strengthens the character.

"My participation in litigation wars has stamped my soul with an imperative to avoid the uncertainties and ambiguities that foster controversy. It has also given me a bias to resolve differences, where possible, by private settlement rather than by adversary litigation, causing me to believe that sometimes even a poor settlement is better than a good lawsuit.

"I have also seen the gospel ideal of service to others being nobly expressed by the uncompensated and even the compensated service of members of the legal profession."[1]

There are lots of what are called lawyer jokes, some of which are valuable to criticize professional characteristics that are deficient. But the legal profession also has characteristics that are noble and essential to a society for which it provides *advocates* and *judges*. I am pleased to see that

---

1. "The Beginning and the End of a Lawyer," *Clark Memorandum,* Spring 2005, 11.

these titles are among those by which our Savior identifies Himself.[2]

Persons in other occupations will have a different list of principal learnings.

It is valuable to analyze our own professional or occupational learning and consider how it has shaped our thinking and our qualifications for future service.

---

2. See Topical Guide, "Jesus Christ, Advocate"; "Jesus Christ, Judge."

Chapter 23

TRANSITION TO
THE APOSTLESHIP

I WAS CALLED AS AN APOSTLE and sustained as a member of the Quorum of the Twelve on April 7, 1984. At that time I was serving as a justice on the Utah Supreme Court. I was probably the first person called to the apostleship while in government service.[1] This posed a problem of transition.

Because of the separation of church and state required by the United States Constitution, which was a response to the founders' knowledge of abuses by authorities exercising both church power and government power, it was essential for me to complete my official responsibilities before

---

1. J. Reuben Clark Jr. was called to the First Presidency in December 1931 while serving as United States ambassador to Mexico. As a result, his calling was not announced and he was not sustained until April 1933. He was ordained an Apostle in October 1934.

Elder Dallin H. Oaks

entering upon my Church service. It required twenty-five days for me to finish the opinions I had been assigned to write for the court and to cast my votes on other cases under consideration where my vote was essential to a majority in our five-judge court.

During my time of continuing to serve as a justice of the Utah Supreme Court while knowing that the rest of my life would be spent in the service of the Lord, I had time for deep reflection on the responsibilities I would soon assume and exercise for the rest of my life. I felt very inadequate and very apprehensive. I took an inventory of my professional credentials, experience, and qualifications and compared them with the kinds of things I thought I would be called upon to do as an Apostle. I asked myself, "Throughout the remainder of your life will you be a lawyer and judge who has been called to be an Apostle, or will you be an Apostle who used to be a lawyer and judge?"

There is a strong tendency in most of us to spend most of our time doing what we feel comfortable in doing—to seek to fulfill our responsibilities through activities in which we feel a sense of mastery or at least familiarity. That tendency is particularly significant when we move from one position to another, especially when the responsibilities of the new position are very different from those of the former one. I knew I must not surrender to that tendency.

The most important parts of my new calling—the only parts really unique in the service of the Lord—were those parts that I knew nothing about, the parts where I would have to start all over at the beginning. I knew that if I concentrated my time on the things that came naturally—the things that I felt qualified to do—I would never measure up as an Apostle. I would always be a former lawyer and judge. That was not what I wanted. I decided that I would focus my efforts on becoming what I had been called to be, not on what I felt qualified to do. I determined that instead of trying to shape my calling to my credentials, I would try to shape myself to my calling.[2]

For the first decade of my service I explained this determination to many different audiences of Church leaders, especially to those who needed a similar change in their own thinking. To mission presidents I issued the challenge to stop thinking of themselves in relation to the occupation from which they had been called and to think of themselves as a leader of missionaries. To missionaries I issued the challenge to stop thinking of themselves as grown-up teenagers or fans of a particular sports team and to see themselves as servants of the Lord Jesus Christ who had been called to do His work in His way.

In the course of recalling this explanation of my transition, I came upon the text of a talk I gave at the twenty-fifth anniversary celebration of the American Indian students who performed at Brigham Young University (a group then called the Lamanite Generation). The analogy I used there, which I thought would be meaningful to them, is also a good expression of what I had been trying to do:

"Would I be a lawyer who had been called to be an Apostle, or would I be an Apostle who used to be a lawyer? Lawyer was my tribe. Apostle was my calling and overriding

---

2. Parts of the preceding three paragraphs are modified from a talk I gave at the Brigham Young University J. Reuben Clark Law School, February 8, 1987. See "Bridges," *Clark Memorandum,* Fall 1988, 12.

loyalty. I have not ceased to be a member of my legal tribe, to honor its wholesome traditions and accomplishments, and to benefit from the education I received in the law. But I have ceased to view myself as a lawyer. I am an Apostle who was educated as a lawyer."[3]

When called to a Church position, we should focus our efforts on being what we are called to _be_, not on what we feel qualified to _do_.

---

3. Talk given at Brigham Young University, Provo, Utah, March 30, 1996.

Chapter 24

UNSELFISH SERVICE

S ERVICE THAT IS GIVEN WITH little or no thought of personal advantage is an ideal to pursue for a lifetime. Like humility, service that is unconscious of self must be learned gradually.

I had not thought that I would be taught unselfish service in law school, but I was. Several of my teachers taught explicitly and by example that lawyering was not just a way to acquire wealth or to secure a position of power or influence. Edward H. Levi, who was my teacher, my dean, and in many ways my mentor, was such an example. His paramount interest was making the law what it ought to be for the good of the people and the country. He taught his students and associates to do the same. He never seemed to me to have any personal interest. I saw him as a man without self-promotion or concern with what we now call political correctness. He was fundamentally grounded in what he believed to be right for those he served.

Shortly after my calling as an Apostle I had another landmark lesson about the deficiency of service that is conscious of self. I spoke to Elder (as he then was) Boyd K. Packer about how inadequate I felt for the calling I had received. He responded with this mild reproof and challenging insight:

"I suppose your feelings are understandable. But you should work for a condition where you will not be preoccupied with yourself and your own feelings of inadequacy and can give your entire concern to others and to the work of the Lord in all the world."

Jesus taught that those who would follow him should deny themselves: "For whosoever will save his life shall lose it: and whosoever will lose his life for my sake shall find it" (Matthew 16:25). Thus, the Lord wants us to teach and minister out of love for Him and for His children, not to fill any need or win any recognition for ourselves. Those who seem to do the Lord's work but actually work for personal gain or recognition are guilty of priestcraft, which the Book of Mormon defines as activities by which "men preach and set themselves up for a light unto the world, that they may get gain and praise of the world; but they seek not the welfare of Zion" (2 Nephi 26:29; see also Alma 1:16).

We promote unselfish service when we praise the work

rather than the person who does it. The Savior provided a great example of this. In giving His people a "commandment . . . that ye search [the writings of Isaiah] diligently," the Savior did not praise that great prophet. His explanation was "for great are the *words* of Isaiah" (3 Nephi 23:1; emphasis added). Similarly, if we praise the words or the work, we bestow recognition on the Master who directed it, not on the servant who seemed to accomplish it.

The Lord teaches us to serve out of love for Him and for His children, not to fill any need or win any recognition for ourselves.

Chapter 25

THE MEANING OF
"REAL INTENT"

I LEARNED THE MEANING OF AN important scriptural term, "real intent" (Moroni 10:4), from an experience I had many years ago.

While I was a stake missionary in Chicago, my companion and I were meeting with a good Christian man who said he had been saved. He seemed to be interested in our message. Although he did not accept our invitation to attend church, he prayed with us and accepted a copy of the Book of Mormon and said he would read it. We were persuaded that he loved the Lord and that he sincerely desired to know about the Book of Mormon. He accepted our challenge to qualify for the promise in Moroni 10:4 but after several weekly meetings insisted that he had received no manifestation of the truth of the Book of Mormon. He also told us that he saw no need to be baptized because he had already been baptized, and, in any event, he had already been saved by accepting Jesus Christ as his personal Savior. We eventually parted in a friendly way, and my companion and I went on to work with others who were more receptive.

I pondered that experience for many years, wondering why this man, who I was sure had asked the Lord with a sincere heart and with faith in Christ, had not received a manifestation of the truth of the Book of Mormon. Finally the understanding came. I had overlooked an essential condition in the promise contained in Moroni 10:4, and this was the step our friend had omitted.

It is not enough to ask with a sincere heart, having faith in Christ. We must also ask with *real intent*. Real intent requires a commitment to act upon the truth when the Lord reveals it. Without real intent, what we are asking the Lord is merely an academic question, meaning that whatever the answer is, it won't affect our behavior. The Lord does not promise to answer an academic question.

I realized that while our investigator sincerely wanted to know whether the Book of Mormon was true, he could not have been praying with real intent. He was convinced that he had already been saved, and he had no intention of being baptized even if he received a manifestation of the truth of the Book of Mormon.

When I learned that lesson, I began to include it in my talks. Soon thereafter I had an impressive confirmation of the principle. A member whose husband had investigated the Church for many years and who had heard me explain this principle in a fireside wrote to me about its effect. She said that her husband had prayed on Friday that something might happen during the fireside that would help him know whether the Church was true. She said he felt I was speaking directly to him on Saturday night. Her letter continued:

"Sunday afternoon he pondered the words 'real intent.' He committed himself to baptism that same day if he could just know it was the right thing to do. He received his answer! After many years of fasting and struggle he finally felt good enough about it to take action, and he was baptized about 7:15 P.M. and is now a member of The Church of Jesus Christ of Latter-day Saints. Afterwards he told me he was glad he did it and he knew it was right."

The key to the answer to this man's prayer is that he finally gave the Lord the necessary commitment to act upon the answer if he received it. That is praying with real intent. His wife's letter continues:

"Now, he will have the great blessing of baptizing [eight-year-old] Julie in a couple of weeks. This is something I have hoped and prayed for, for several years."[1]

What I learned from these experiences is that we must always pray with real intent—a commitment to act upon the answer—if our questions and our prayers are to be answered.

---

1. Letter, February 2, 1987.

The same principle applies to repentance, which must be undertaken with "full purpose of heart" (the same thing as real intent for this purpose) if we are to be accepted and forgiven (Jacob 6:5; 3 Nephi 10:6; 18:32; see also D&C 42:25). In other words, it is not enough to go through the other steps to obtain forgiveness for a sin if you are doing it only to qualify for a temple recommend or a missionary call and you have no intention of refraining from your sinful behavior once you have gained the temporary advantage. That is not repenting with full purpose of heart, and the Lord makes no promise of forgiveness in that circumstance. This requirement of true commitment is included in the Savior's loving invitation to come unto Him. He told the Nephites, "Come unto me with full purpose of heart, and I will receive you" (3 Nephi 12:24).

In order to ask with real intent or to act with full purpose of heart, we must always make an accompanying commitment.

Chapter 26

REFUSING REQUESTS

BEGINNING WITH MY EXPERIENCES as president of Brigham Young University and intensifying with the demands on a General Authority, I have had to refuse many requests from people who wanted to meet with me or have me intervene in their behalf. Though inevitable because of the number of requests and the need to respect lines of authority and the agency of others involved, my refusals have been painful on both sides. I have had to learn how to say no in a way that tries to minimize pain and also tries to be helpful.

Following are quotations from just a few of the hundreds of letters I have sent as I have learned how to respond to such requests.

1. One of about sixty BYU department chairmen sought an hour-long meeting with his new president to discuss instructional techniques, grading options, and other matters that concerned him. I replied that I could not do this when I was "forced to do [so many] things a few minutes at a time, here and there." I asked him to put his thoughts in a memorandum I could study.[1] Asking persons to put their thoughts in writing and send them to me is a practice I followed after learning that many who wanted to meet with me or talk with me on the phone expected me to write out their thoughts for them. I had to learn that I did not have time to do this.

2. A parent wrote to me, as BYU president, requesting that I meet and give a "pep talk" to his nine-year-old son. I replied that "the duties of my office require me to do so many things that no one else can do, that I find it necessary to delegate whatever can be done by others."[2] The principle of delegation is one every prominent and busy person must learn and apply.

3. After I was called as an Apostle, a young man who had violated a commandment for two years asked to meet with me so he could "be cleansed from this terrible sin." In reply I asked him to see his bishop, giving this explanation that every experienced leader must give frequently:

1. Letter, August 1971.
2. Letter, April 1980.

"[Your bishop] is the one who can help you do what you need to do in order for the atoning sacrifice of Jesus Christ to work its purpose in your life. No mortal can cleanse you, but the Savior can do so if you keep His commandments. You need to see your bishop for this purpose, not me or any other General Authority."[3]

If that principle were learned by all Latter-day Saints, it would materially reduce the mail that comes to Church headquarters. The First Presidency has repeatedly taught this in letters read in sacrament meetings. Their 2008 letter includes these explanations:

"The Lord, in His wisdom, has organized His Church so that every member has a bishop or branch president and a stake, district, or mission president, who serve as spiritual advisers and temporal counselors. We have the utmost confidence in the wisdom and judgment of these priesthood leaders. By reason of their callings, local leaders are entitled to the spirit of discernment and inspiration to enable them to counsel members within their jurisdiction.

"Accordingly, in most cases correspondence from members will be referred back to their local leaders for handling. Stake presidents who have need for further clarification about doctrinal or procedural issues may write to the First Presidency in behalf of their members."[4]

---

3. Letter, May 1990.

4. First Presidency letter, March 18, 2008. The First Presidency's letter of October 6, 2010, is even more direct.

4. In declining a member's request to talk with me about a variety of circumstances in the writer's family, I gave this reason:

"We find that when a member of the Quorum of the Twelve sees members about personal matters, they are then quite unable to get assistance from their bishop or their stake president (who understandably react that the matter is being handled by the Twelve and they should not touch it). That is quite damaging to the member because the member of the Quorum of the Twelve is likely to be in another part of the world and inaccessible when the member needs the next step in help that often needs to be ongoing."

I added this counsel, which applies in so many circumstances of discord in family relationships:

"The kind of problem you describe in your letter is the kind that often requires a long time to resolve. The Savior's way requires patience and ample opportunity for persons (even persons who are at fault) to use their own agency to make the choices necessary for their growth. In the meantime, others endure painful circumstances and have to exercise almost superhuman patience. But that is the Lord's way, and the Church and His servants have no way to compel otherwise. If we cannot be patient with the existing circumstance, the processes of the civil law are the only compulsory processes available to us."[5]

5. Letter, about 1988.

5. A letter from a prison inmate requested intervention in his divorced wife's attempt to cancel their temple sealing. I assured him of the Lord's love for him and of His willingness to guide him in his future life. I continued:

"But you go too far when you conclude that if only you have enough faith He will 'heal [your] relationship and marriage' with your former wife. The Lord honors our agency— hers as well as yours. He will not override the agency of another person, no matter how much faith we have in Him. Consequently, I believe you should direct your prayers in the matter of the temple cancellation she seeks to ask for guidance in what the Lord would have you do for her benefit and then put your life in His hands to guide you in what you should do in the future. I believe that is the path of growth for you and that is the way for you to realize the happiness you seek.

"I note that you will soon be paroled. I pray that you will be strong as you continue your therapy and as you embark upon the difficult task of getting reintegrated into society and reestablishing wholesome contacts with your family members and former friends. In this you should seek and follow the counsel of your bishop. He is the Lord's servant and will guide you according to the inspiration of the Lord for your benefit."[6]

6. Letter, July 2010.

6. A mother who felt shabbily treated by officials in a Church education institution wrote for intervention or comfort from an Apostle. In responding I applied what I have learned about the value of speaking directly, though hopefully with kindness.

"In each of those circumstances [you have recited] there are two sides—what you have told me, and what I would be told if I questioned others about the same circumstances. I know there are two sides, since I have had a whole lifetime of experience (in my profession, in my assignments at BYU, and in the Church) in hearing the kind of difficulties recited in your letter. My admiration for someone who encounters those kinds of difficulties and just keeps forging ahead, as you have done, is very great.

"You asked me to reply to you and to counsel you. I am glad to do so, but I am conscious that what I can do by letter or even in person is quite limited. It is clear that I cannot declare that you have always been right in what you have done and that those with whom you dealt have always been wrong. I cannot do that without speaking to the others and going into a lengthy review of a variety of different circumstances. That would go far beyond my calling and would not be good for anyone.

"All that I can really do in the circumstances (which is not as much as your own bishop, family, and friends can do) is to counsel you to keep on trying and to exercise the kind of patience we are called upon to exercise with those around us."[7]

General Church leaders cannot meet with or intervene for all who request their help. For the Church to function as it must, members should seek solutions through personal inspiration or counsel from their local leaders.

7. Letter, November 1991.

Chapter 27

RECOGNIZING
REVELATION

R EVELATION FROM GOD to man comes for different purposes and in different ways.[1] It should be a reality for every Latter-day Saint, because each has the gift of the Holy Ghost. Nevertheless, some have difficulty recognizing revelation when it comes.

A returned missionary, married with three children, wrote me, "If only I could *know* that God exists!" Despite his prayers and his years of scripture study, he said, he still lacked the certainty of the kind of revelation he craved.[2]

My reply describes what I learned from pondering how I could help him:

---

1. See Dallin H. Oaks, "Revelation," *New Era,* September 1982, 38–46.
2. Letter, October 5, 1986.

"It seems to me that your major concern is that you do not think you are receiving an answer to your prayers for a testimony. At one point you say, 'Why has there never been communication between God and myself—one to one?' At another place you say that you have prayed and 'nothing has ever happened.'

"I wonder what you expect as an answer to your prayers? I am reminded of the example of the prophet Elijah, who *had* heard the voice of the Lord, but who was taught on one occasion that the communications from the Lord come as 'a still small voice' (1 Kings 19:12).

"Perhaps your prayers have been answered again and again, but you have had your expectations fixed on a sign so grand or a voice so loud that you think you have had no answer."[3]

I could also have referred to two examples from which we learn other ways that revelation comes. Oliver Cowdery prayed for a witness of the truth of the Book of Mormon translation work and received a revelation he did not recognize at the time. Later the Lord told Oliver by revelation through the Prophet Joseph Smith:

"Did I not speak peace to your mind concerning the matter? What greater witness can you have than from God?" (D&C 6:23).

---

3. Letter, October 1986.

Much later, Joseph Smith gave this description of another form of revelation:

"A person may profit by noticing the first intimation of the spirit of revelation; for instance, when you feel pure intelligence flowing into you, it may give you sudden strokes of ideas . . . and thus by learning the Spirit of God and understanding it, you may grow into the principle of revelation, until you become perfect in Christ Jesus."[4]

On the question of testimony, I reminded the Church member who wrote me that "people have different spiritual gifts. As you know . . . some have the gift of *knowing* that 'Jesus Christ is the Son of God,' and 'to others it is given to believe on their words, that they also might have eternal life if they continue faithful' (D&C 46:13–14). Perhaps that scripture is the ultimate answer to your question. It surely shows that eternal life is also available to those 'who believe on their words.'"[5]

Revelation comes in different ways, and we should be open to recognize and receive it, even if it comes as "a still small voice" (1 Kings 19:12).

---

4. *Joseph Smith*, Teachings of Presidents of the Church series (Salt Lake City: The Church of Jesus Christ of Latter-day Saints, 2007), 132.

5. Letter, October 1986.

Chapter 28

LABELING AND TIMING

THE POWER OF IDEAS GENERALLY can be measured in terms of their importance, which means the pervasiveness or breadth of their effect. The more things an idea can influence, the more powerful it is. For example, some ideas can be likened to a rock flying through the air. Within its own trajectory and along its own small perimeter, a flying rock can have quite an impact. But outside its trajectory and perimeter, it has no impact at all. In contrast, even a gentle breeze is very powerful. It will benefit millions by turning windmills, moving sailboats, and drying hay. Powerful ideas are like that.

Two powerful ideas that I learned later in life involve the effect of labeling and the vital importance of timing.

I.

In many different settings I have observed how persons can label or characterize themselves or allow others to label or characterize them in ways that can effectively retard their progress. We should be careful not to label or define ourselves by some temporary quality. The only *single* quality that should characterize us is that each of us is a son or daughter of God. That fact transcends all other characteristics.

Yet there are those among us who choose to define or label themselves by some temporary characteristic, such as occupation, appearance, honors, athletic ability, or fame.

When we choose to define or label ourselves by some characteristic that is temporary or trivial in eternal terms, we de-emphasize what is most important about us and overemphasize what is relatively unimportant. This label can lead us down the wrong path and hinder our eternal progress. For example, a person who defines himself as an underachiever tends to look for—or encourage others to look for—things that interpret his behavior in those terms. That has a very different consequence than if he and others look on his quality of underachieving as simply a temporary tendency that needs to be disciplined in the course of seeking graduation, employment, or eternal life. We should always remember that we are sons or daughters of Heavenly Parents, seeking to qualify for our eternal heirship under that parentage.[1]

II.

Learning the importance of timing has been hard for me. I tend to think that whenever I have an idea it is time to proceed on it, and whenever there is a problem the sooner I confront it the better. When a task needs doing, I tend to think that it should be done now.

I have had to learn that in most big decisions, what is most important is to *do the right thing.* Second, and only slightly behind the first, is to *do the right thing at the right time.* If we do the right thing at the wrong time, we can be frustrated and ineffective. We can even be confused about whether we have made the right choice when what was wrong was not our choice but our timing.

Elder Neal A. Maxwell helped me understand the role of faith in this issue of timing. Faith means not only to trust in God's will and way of doing things but also to trust in his timing.[2] We should not try to impose our desired timing on the Lord. He has revealed that "to every thing there is a season, and a time to every purpose under the heaven" (Ecclesiastes 3:1) and that "all things must come to pass in

---

1. This paragraph is based on part of my devotional message "Be Wise," at BYU–Idaho, Rexburg, Idaho, November 7, 2006.
2. See Neal A. Maxwell, *Even As I Am* (Salt Lake City: Deseret Book, 1982), 93.

their time" (D&C 64:32). The Lord is in charge, and He will do His own work in His own time.

I have also learned that the principle of the Lord's timing illustrates the need for continuing revelation, which is the means by which the Lord administers His timing. It is not enough that we are under call, or even that we are going in the right direction. The timing must be right, and if the time is not right, our actions must be adjusted to the Lord's timing as revealed by His servants. The Lord's timing also applies to the important events of our personal lives, such as birth, marriage, and death.[3]

The way we label ourselves—by eternal or temporary characteristics—and our acceptance or rejection of the Lord's timing are powerful ideas that will shape our actions and affect our happiness.

---

3. See my talk titled "Timing," *Ensign,* October 2003, 10–17.

Chapter 29

TITHING BLESSINGS

SINCE MY YOUTH I HAVE ALWAYS paid a full tithing. I learned this principle from my mother. Again and again I have experienced the fulfillment of the Lord's promise that He would "open you [tithe payers] the windows of heaven, and pour you out a blessing, that there shall not be room enough to receive it. And I will rebuke the devourer for your sakes, and he shall not destroy the fruits of your ground" (Malachi 3:10–11).

In a general conference talk on tithing I described my mother's teaching:

"During World War II, my widowed mother supported her three young children on a schoolteacher's salary that was meager. When I became conscious that we went without some desirable things because we didn't have enough money, I asked my mother why she paid so much of her salary as tithing. I have never forgotten her explanation: 'Dallin, there might be some people who can get along without paying tithing, but we can't. The Lord has chosen to take your father and leave me to raise you children. I cannot do that without the blessings of the Lord, and I obtain those blessings by paying an honest tithing. When I pay my tithing, I have the Lord's promise that he will bless us, and we must have those blessings if we are to get along.'"[1]

To show our gratitude for these blessings and to illustrate the desirability of paying tithing, whenever June and I or our children experienced an unexpected advantage, such as extra income or reduced expenses, we would declare it "a tithing blessing." Our children have continued this practice. When they or their families are benefited by some important happening, they declare it "a tithing blessing." This helps children recognize and acknowledge the blessings of paying tithing.

I also encourage the identification of "tithing blessings" when I teach at Church conferences. I believe most Church members who don't enjoy the blessings of paying tithing know what the commandment is. They don't need a sermon

---

1. "Tithing," *Ensign,* May 1994, 33.

on its importance. They just need increased faith to pay it. Convincing testimonies of "tithing blessings" will strengthen their faith and their performance.

Those who place faith in the Lord's promises pay a full tithing and are blessed for doing so.

Chapter 30

SINS AND MISTAKES

ONE OF THE MANY THINGS I learned later in my life is the difference between sins and mistakes. I wish I had known this difference earlier, since it would have helped me as a parent and also as a gospel teacher. After gaining this insight I made it the subject of a talk at Brigham Young University in August 1994. The fact that I didn't gain this insight until after I became a full-time teacher of the gospel persuades me that others may have missed this difference also. I therefore include these paragraphs from that talk, as subsequently published in the *Ensign:*

"I wish to reason about a basic principle given in modern revelation but not as well understood or applied as it should be. . . .

"Three verses of the Doctrine and Covenants identify an

important contrast between sins and mistakes. I had never pondered these verses until . . . I was reading the Doctrine and Covenants for the 15th or 20th time. Their direction came to my mind with such freshness and impact that I thought they might have been newly inserted in my book. That is the way with prayerful study of the scriptures. The scriptures do not change, but we do, and so the same scriptures can give us new insights every time we read them.

"The 20th section of the Doctrine and Covenants, given the same month the Church was organized, is the basic revelation on Church government. It contains one verse giving this important direction: 'Any member of the church of Christ transgressing, or being overtaken in a fault, shall be dealt with as the scriptures direct' (v. 80). The clear implication of this verse is that 'transgressing' is different from being 'overtaken in a fault,' but that either type of action is to be dealt with as the scriptures direct.

"The scriptures contain various directions for dealing with members, but the key direction is contained in two verses in the November 1831 revelation given as the preface to the book that is now the Doctrine and Covenants. . . .

"'Inasmuch as they erred it might be made known; . . .

"'And inasmuch as they sinned they might be chastened, that they might repent' (vv. 25, 27).

"In these verses, 'transgressing' is different from 'being at fault,' and 'to err' is different than 'to sin.' I believe that in these scriptures *sin* and *transgression* mean the same thing.

Similarly, 'to err' and 'to be at fault' are also equivalent. In referring to this second category, I will use the more familiar description: 'to make a mistake.'

"Both sins and mistakes can hurt us and both require attention, but the scriptures direct a different treatment. Chewing on a live electrical cord or diving headfirst into water of uncertain depth are mistakes that should be made known so that they can be avoided. Violations of the commandments of God are sins that require chastening and repentance. In the treatment process we should not require repentance for mistakes, but we are commanded to preach the necessity of repentance for sins. . . .

"The distinction between sins and mistakes is important to our actions in the realm of politics and public policy debates. We have seen some very bitter finger-pointing among Latter-day Saints who disagree with one another on the policies a government should follow, the political parties they should support, or the persons they should elect as public servants. Such disagreements are inevitable in representative government. But it is not inevitable that they would result in the personal denunciations and bitter feelings described in the press or encountered in personal conversations.

"We put political disagreements in the appropriate context when we remember that even if our political adversaries are making the wrong choice (as we suppose), that is generally a matter of error (mistake) rather than transgression (sin). (Of course, there are some public policies so intertwined with moral issues that there may be only one morally right position, but that is rare.) . . .

"Even though they have taught their children all of the commandments and principles they need for righteous and provident living, parents are still susceptible to the serious error of failing to distinguish between mistakes and sins. If well-meaning parents call teenagers to repentance for teenagers' numerous mistakes, they may dilute the effect of chastisement and reduce the impact of repentance for the category of teenage sins that really require it. . . .

"Sins result from willful disobedience of laws we have received by explicit teaching or by the Spirit of Christ, which teaches every man the general principles of right and wrong. For sins, the remedy is to chasten and encourage repentance.

"Mistakes result from ignorance of the laws of God or the workings of the universe or people he has created. For mistakes, the remedy is to correct the mistake, not to condemn the individual." [1]

There is an important difference between a *sin*, which requires repentance, and a *mistake*, which need only be corrected.

---

1. "Sins and Mistakes," *Ensign,* October 1996, 62–67.

Chapter 31

LOOKING INTO
THE FUTURE

OVER MY ADULT LIFE I HAVE learned some disadvantages and some advantages of trying to look into the future.

A scriptural caution in the Book of Mormon illustrates a *disadvantage* of trying to look into the future. The prophet Jacob described a people who "despised the words of plainness . . . and sought for things . . . they could not understand" (Jacob 4:14). He said this caused them to fall because when persons are "looking beyond the mark" God takes away plainness and gives them what they sought—things they cannot understand.

I think of this scriptural caution against "looking beyond the mark" when I receive letters asking about such things as how we should plan to build up the New Jerusalem or seeking to know the exact position in the celestial kingdom of a person who has lived a good life but never married or of a married couple in which the husband is (or is not) sealed to more than one woman. I don't know the answers to these and many other such questions. What I do know is that when we are uncertain about some gospel principle or future event, it is usually best to act on what we do know and trust in a loving Heavenly Father to give us further knowledge when we really need it. If we seek a firmer understanding and a better practice of the basic principles of the gospel while trusting in God for the outcome—not seeking to know details we have not been given and probably could not understand if we had—we will be given the peace to live with any uncertainties.

A memory of a father-son conversation of many years ago illustrates the importance of acting on what we do know and trusting in the Lord to give us further knowledge when future events make it really necessary. One of my sons remembers that he came to me with one of those awkward and difficult questions about the history of the Church. When he related this experience, he could not even tell me what the question was, and that is significant in itself. But it was the answer that was significant to him and had stayed with him over the years. He told me I had said, "I don't know, son, but what I do know is that Joseph Smith was a prophet of God."

Although there are some disadvantages in trying to look

too far into the future, the *advantages* of doing so (or the *disadvantages* of failing to do so) are probably more common. I gave a talk on this subject at Brigham Young University titled "Where Will It Lead?" There I described some societal trends and personal choices that will surely lead to great problems in the future. My many examples included "the terrible [future] consequences of partaking of anything that can be addictive."[1] Here I will share an additional example that has contributed to my personal learning on the importance of looking into the future and asking "Where will it lead?"

For much of my professional life, beginning with my service as BYU president, I have received recommendations and counsel on decisions I had to make. Sometimes different persons gave very different counsel. Similarly, I received many letters from students, faculty, alumni, and parents giving advice on what the university should do. Again, the advice was sometimes quite varied. I continue to receive such letters in my capacity as a General Authority.

The lesson I learned early, which has been extremely valuable to me, involves looking to the future. In determining what weight I should attach to particular advice, I ask myself, "What responsibility will this person have in the future for the effects of the advice now being offered?" Then, I

---

1. In *Brigham Young University 2004–2005 Devotional and Fireside Speeches* (Provo, Utah: Brigham Young University, 2005), 237–48; *BYU Magazine,* Summer 2005, 33–40.

attach the greatest weight to advice that comes from persons who will have to live with (such as by administering) the consequences of the decision. I give the lightest weight to counsel from those who are just sharing a thought or a preference or a bias for whose consequences they will not need to accept any responsibility.

During the week I wrote these words, I heard President Thomas S. Monson make a comment that expresses this same wisdom. In a discussion of various alternatives for a Church policy, he observed, with the wisdom that comes from experience (in this case, that of a United States Navy man in World War II), that "no one takes care of a ship like those who must sail in it."

Trying to look into the future risks the disadvantage of "looking beyond the mark" but has the advantages that come from asking "Where will it lead?"

Chapter 32

PRINCIPLES VERSUS PREFERENCES

I N OUR PERSONAL CHOICES WE should be conscious of the important difference between choices that should be governed by principles (including the commandments of the Lord) and choices that can be based on personal preferences. How to recognize and apply this difference is something we learn by experience. The result of this learning is wisdom, which the scriptures teach us to learn and seek (Alma 32:12; D&C 6:7).

The difference between choices based on principles and those based on preferences is especially important for parents, who should stand fast on the principles they teach their children but at the same time be flexible on matters that can be left to their personal preferences and the preferences of their children. For example, every family has some dos and don'ts—rules and procedures that govern how the family works together. Some of these are based on eternal principles, established by the commandments of God and taught by His servants. Other family rules and procedures— probably most of them—are merely expressions of the preferences of the parents and the children.

For example, how we dress is a matter of both principle and preference. When we go to worship, whether in sacrament meeting or in the temple, we should choose clothing and footwear that shows our respect for the act of worship and for Him whom we worship. Personal preference obviously applies to many of our choices, but if our choices cause us to select clothing or footwear that is similar to what we would wear to the beach or to do our household or barnyard chores, we have violated a principle that forbids casualness or commonness when we come into the house of the Lord.

It is important that rules based on principles not be confused with rules based on preferences. Children need to understand that certain parental directions are matters of right and wrong, which should be the same in all families, but that many family rules and procedures are matters of parental preference. Knowing this distinction will prevent confusion when they see differences between how their family does things and how those same things are done in the families of other faithful Latter-day Saints.

Understanding the difference between principles and preferences will also help a newly married husband and wife reconcile the different preferences of the families in which they were raised. While holding fast to principles, a newly married couple will need to decide which preferences they will adopt for their own family. I remember making this distinction many years ago. As a matter of principle, June and I determined that we would have a kneeling family prayer each morning. On matters of preference, we made individual choices that responded to the intensity of the other's desires. Thus, on a relatively trivial matter, I remember yielding to the Dixon family's Thanksgiving practice of *moist* turkey dressing instead of the *dry* dressing my family always preferred.

Recognizing the difference between principle and practice, and its application to the many choices a newly married couple must make, can save some difficulty and heartache. Similarly, recognizing this difference in other choices of our lives can also be helpful.

Some personal choices should be based on principles, and some can be based on preferences.

Chapter 33

CAUTION IN SHARING SPIRITUAL EXPERIENCES

AFTER I SPOKE IN GENERAL CONFERENCE about the way I was miraculously preserved from danger in an attempted robbery on the streets of Chicago,[1] a church member wrote asking why our leaders seldom speak of miraculous spiritual experiences. He said this caused some members to wonder whether such experiences—common in the earlier years of the Restoration—still occurred. My reply, including what I learned by pondering this question, is summarized below.

Two early revelations direct caution in speaking of sacred things:

"Remember that that which cometh from above is

---

1. "Bible Stories and Personal Protection," *Ensign,* Nov. 1992, 39–40.

sacred, and must be spoken with care, and by constraint of the Spirit; and in this there is no condemnation" (D&C 63:64).

Similarly, after again promising that signs would follow those who believed, the Savior declared:

"But a commandment I give unto them, that they shall not boast themselves of these things, neither speak them before the world; for these things are given unto you for your profit and for salvation" (D&C 84:73).

Because of these scriptural directions and for other reasons, leaders and members of the Church usually refrain from speaking publicly about miracles or sacred spiritual experiences. In this we are like Mary, who "kept all these things, and pondered them in her heart" (Luke 2:19).

There are exceptions. We speak of sacred things when the Spirit prompts us strongly to do so. When this occurs, it is usually for an intimate audience, such as immediate family or trusted close associates.

To those who wonder if miracles and other sacred spiritual experiences still occur, I affirm that they do but concede that our members seem to share them less frequently than in earlier times. Why?

The best explanation is our current understanding of the scriptural directions I have quoted above. Also of influence is the ascendancy of the rational over the supernatural in our education, our state of mind, and our conversation. We also hesitate to share precious spiritual experiences when that may lead to unfriendly attempts to ridicule them or explain them away on the rational grounds so common in our secular societies. Perhaps our understanding of the Savior's admonition not to cast our pearls before swine (Matthew 7:6) contributes to this hesitancy. In contrast, in societies where the rational has not prevailed over the supernatural to such an extent, spiritual experiences are reported more often and shared more readily.[2]

I hope that our Latter-day Saint tendency to say little about modern miracles and much about the visible fruits of our faith and the commendable accomplishments of more prominent Church members does not mislead anyone into overlooking the miracles and the rich but private spiritual experiences of less well-known Latter-day Saints.

Because of scriptural directions, reinforced by the skepticism of modern secular societies, Latter-day Saints are cautious about sharing miraculous spiritual experiences.

2. For example, see Eric B. Shumway, *Tongan Saints: Legacy of Faith* (Laie, Hawaii: Institute for Polynesian Studies, 1991).

Chapter 34

DEATH OF A SPOUSE

I LEARNED WHAT IT WAS LIKE to suffer the death of a beloved spouse. Others have had or will have the same experience. I share here what I learned, knowing that only some of my experiences and conclusions are true for everyone. On this subject, much is individual.

When we lose a spouse, we are usually unaware of how deeply wounded we are. For a time we do not function well, physically or mentally. We should not make major decisions until we are mostly whole again. The required time will differ. For me, it was about a year before I could trust myself with a major personal decision.

As I look back on my personal healing from June's death, I believe there were three major memories on which I relied

Cemetery, July 1998

for comfort. I sometimes referred to these memories as my "three-legged stool."

First was my absolute faith in the reality of the Resurrection. Because my faith and knowledge on this subject are not unique to me, I will say no more about them here.[1]

Second was my memory that although I had not been a perfect husband and wished I had done many things better, I had never betrayed June's trust or violated our marriage covenants.

---

1. As soon as I felt able to trust my emotions, I gave a general conference talk that included my testimony of the Resurrection. See "The Gospel in Our Lives," *Ensign,* May 2002, 34–35.

Third was my memory of caring for her personally during her last illness, doing all she requested that was within my power. We were blessed that she was able to fight her battle with cancer at home (except for one day of hospitalization), surrounded by her loved ones. We had ample time to discuss what we could see of the future and to receive a measure of closure about it.

Those three memories all related to what preceded June's death. The fourth major influence in my healing was the grief I experienced after her death and what I did to draw it out, process it, and reduce it to the point that it was not disabling. Each surviving spouse will do this in his or her own way. For me, the process of drawing out my grief and reducing it to a tolerable level was importantly associated with my writing a history of June's life. This year-long task began as a sweet diversion to fulfill her desire that our posterity would know her as they would know me. Fortunately, preparing her history turned out to be the essential and culminating step in my healing from the wounds caused by her death.

I had abundant sources. I had June's journals and mine. I had the written contributions of our six children, and I had some choice recollections and tributes in the hundreds of letters received after her death. Evening after evening I read these sources and relived our forty-seven and a half years together (including our one and a half years of courtship). I would read and weep, write and weep. This sweet experience not only resulted in a lengthy history privately published for our family but also drew out and soothed my grief. I undertook this history as my final mortal service for her, but it surely turned out to be most essential for me.

Others will have other activities to help them work through their essential period of grief. Whatever the activity, my experience persuades me that it should include some organized review of the life of the spouse and it should be something that can be concluded to signify the completion of this intense period of grief. For me that end point was the completion of June's history and its delivery to our children and grandchildren just before the first anniversary of her death. Soon thereafter the Spirit whispered that it was time for me to stop grieving and get on with my life. "To every thing there is a season, and a time to every purpose under the heaven" (Ecclesiastes 3:1).

When wounded by the death of a spouse, we must have time for grieving and for activities to assist it. Then, in time, we must acknowledge our healing and get on with our lives.

Chapter 35

SECOND MARRIAGE

W HETHER A PERSON WHO has lost a spouse enters into a second marriage is a very personal decision. It depends on many individual circumstances, including the ages of the prospective marriage partners and children, financial implications, and even what is known about the feelings of the deceased spouse. In the hope of benefiting others who decide (as I did) to remarry, I share here some of what I learned as I experienced some of the issues involved in a second marriage.

What I learned is related to my personal circumstances. June and I had been married forty-six years at the time of her death. I was then sixty-six years old. We had six children, all married, and twenty-three grandchildren.

Two very important things that helped me through the

adjustments of remarriage happened before June's death. In detail they were unique to our circumstances, but they are mentioned here because they involved principles that will apply to many.

First, June approved of my remarrying. As I mentioned earlier, during her year-long battle with cancer she came to realize that she would die before me. I was never willing to discuss my remarrying, but she frequently told our four daughters that she knew I would need to remarry and that when that time came they should help me find a companion who would fit well into our family, and welcome her. That was her wise preparation, and it proved very important to all of us. I did not begin to look for a wife until all my daughters had come to me individually and told me they were ready for me to remarry. They did not want me to be alone and were emotionally ready for me to proceed. My remarrying was not a problem for our two sons.

Second, without any anticipation of June's predeceasing me, I had kept records throughout our marriage of the gifts and inheritances she received from her parents, including what we purchased with those resources. I was, therefore, in a position to give our children their inheritance from their mother (and her parents) within a year following her death. This was done by transfers of property that had monetary value and by loving division of possessions of sentiment. I made this early distribution so that when the time came for me to remarry, none of the children would have any of the fear I had sometimes observed (as a lawyer or judge or Church leader) that the "new wife" would inherit some of "Mother's property." I wanted that potential concern eliminated long before I remarried and entered into an appropriate prenuptial agreement with a new wife. It was.

The most important decision in remarriage—eternally important and highly personal—is obviously the identity of the second spouse. For Latter-day Saints it is the subject of careful study ("due diligence," some would call it) and fervent prayer. To apply a familiar description, you study it out as if it all depended on you, and you pray as if it all depended on the Lord.

I have had many inquiries about how I found a second wife, including one from a man who wrote asking me to describe my plan of action. My reply to him contains most of what I feel to share here.

"I had no 'plan of action,' except to pray for guidance. After about two years I was feeling strong pressure from my daughters, confirmed by my own feeling, that it was time to look for a companion. At that point I made some discreet inquiries among some associates, and with the help of the inspiration of the Lord, I was soon introduced to Kristen."[1]

In my visible position as a General Authority, I felt it inappropriate to date publicly. My time of getting acquainted with Kristen was spent in the presence of family—my

1. Letter, January 14, 2011.

Dallin and Kristen Oaks

children, my siblings, June's siblings, and Kristen's family members. I followed the familiar wisdom that it is wise to observe a potential marriage partner in a variety of circumstances. We and our family members came to know one another, and by this means I was blessed with the approval of all six of our children before I proposed to Kristen. Those who knew Kristen McMain then, and those who have come to know Kristen M. Oaks now, easily recognize why she was the ideal woman to become part of our family and to stand beside me in the great responsibilities of my calling.

I will mention only a few considerations that influenced my decision, some in the realm of reason and some in the realm of revelation. Kristen's many years of being single, her

146

service as a missionary (in Japan), her doctoral degree from Brigham Young University (in education), and her intelligence, faithfulness, skills as a speaker and teacher, and her loving outreach to others[2] ideally fitted her for the responsibilities that came to her with our marriage. In the way I was led to meet her, in the answer to my prayers for guidance, and in the sacred assurance I received of June's approval, I had the revelatory confirmation I sought.

It was also important to both of us that Kristen felt comfortable about becoming a "second wife." She understood the eternal doctrine of relationships. She was becoming part of an existing eternal family unit, and she has always been eager to honor and include June. In tribute to June she often says, "I am so thankful for the influence of a righteous woman who refined Dallin and the children into the husband and family I love today."

I have learned from many letters received since my remarriage that many who have lost a spouse have questions about the effects of remarriage on family relationships in the eternities to come. There are so many different circumstances involving parents and children, and so little is known about the circumstances of the next life, that it is not possible to give answers to most questions. Some gospel doctrines are revealed only in part. Often, because we do not

---

2. Her fine book, *A Single Voice* (Salt Lake City: Deseret Book, 2008), which I urged her to write to help single Church members and Church leaders, is ample evidence of these important qualifications.

have these doctrines in their entirety, we cannot tell how they will apply to our individual circumstances.

What we do know is sufficient for our mortal decisions. We know that we have a loving Heavenly Father and a loving Savior, Jesus Christ. We trust in the efficacy of temple covenants that have been honored by those who entered them. We trust in the divine plan of salvation and its loving Author. We know that the agency (power of choice) God has given us is a fundamental eternal principle, which He will not violate by forcing any of His children into family relationships they do not choose. We trust in God that all of this, including a second marriage in His temple, will, when covenants are honored, result in the greatest possible happiness for all concerned.

Whether a person who has lost a spouse enters into a second marriage is a very personal decision, depending on many individual circumstances. I was blessed with abundant assistance and guidance, which led me to an ideal companion.

Chapter 36

SHAKING HANDS AT
STAKE CONFERENCES

E ARLY IN MY SERVICE AS A General Authority I learned
that I should shake hands with persons in the congre-
gation—as many as possible—before the stake conference
meeting began. I needed this personal interaction to help
me with the talk I would give, and I soon learned that, for
many, this experience would be remembered long after they
had forgotten what I said in my talk.

My first stake conference assignment after June's death
in July 1998 took place just a month later. I shook hands as
usual. Years later I received this precious letter, which confirmed the importance of my greeting members and investi-
gators before that stake conference:

"I had been meeting with the missionaries for several
months and just didn't feel completely convinced that all

they were teaching me was true. It was in early September, well, maybe late August, that they informed me that one of the Lord's apostles would be visiting Prescott, Arizona (my hometown), and speaking at something they called 'stake conference.' As you would imagine, they invited me to go. Although I hate to admit it, I was more skeptical than anything else. I had wanted so badly for the things they were teaching me to be true, because they sounded so wonderful and I was so unhappy. But it just sounded so absurd to believe there were living apostles. I did eventually decide to go. I was so curious what this 'apostle' would be like or have to say. I remember thinking that if the pastors or ministers of the churches I had previously been attending seemed to think they were just a little bit better than I was, surely someone claiming to be an apostle wouldn't think twice about those he was preaching to. How wrong I was.

"I can't say I remember anything you said in your talk. Oh how I wish I did. But I do remember the care and concern in your voice and how you tried to apply what you were saying to everyone there, from youngest to oldest and everyone in between. I do remember when you went around and shook everyone's hand, and how when you came to me, you looked directly in my eyes. I had never seen eyes like that before, so pure and full of joy. I knew I wished that mine would look like that because I knew how happy I would feel inside if they did. (Isn't it amazing what can be communicated in just a split second?!) So I listened to the rest of your

Meeting Church members, Korea, 2010

talk and felt great. I knew right afterwards the missionaries would come up and ask me what I thought and probably ask me about being baptized. Although I felt good, I still felt a little uneasy. . . .

"Elder Oaks, since I was a little girl I have always thought that one of the worst things that could happen in life would be to have your spouse die. At the end of your talk, as the closing hymn was being sung I flipped through the program and read the little excerpt they had written about you. It said this was your first speaking assignment since the death of your wife. . . . Just then I felt the Spirit rush over me as I realized that anyone whose eyes could look like yours did, [so soon] after such a tragedy, had to be part of something miraculous, and I knew it must be this Church. I went and

151

found the missionaries, told them I wanted to be baptized as soon as possible, and was baptized a few weeks later."[1]

It is in our personal interactions with one another that we are most likely to find the influence and transforming power of the Spirit.

---

1. Letter, September 22, 2003.

Chapter 37

GOOD FRUITS FROM
UNLIKELY SOURCES

THE PROPHET JOSEPH SMITH declared, "I never told you I was perfect; but there is no error in the revelations which I have taught."[1] Of necessity, the Lord does His work through imperfect persons, which should reassure each of us.

From two experiences, more than twenty years apart, I have learned that the Lord sometimes uses even sinful persons to bring good into the lives of His children.

In 1978 the Brigham Young University Young Ambassadors group received a warm reception during their performances in the Soviet Union. My publicized comments to that effect produced a letter from a member of the Church

---

1. *Joseph Smith,* Teachings of Presidents of the Church series (Salt Lake City: The Church of Jesus Christ of Latter-day Saints, 2007), 522.

who had also traveled in the USSR and had seen many of the good things that had been done under that communist government. The writer said: "Strange how 'corrupt' trees do bring forth good fruit, and figs spring forth from thistles. Tragic how we really understand so little."[2]

I replied: "I suppose we can understand that when we see something through the perspective of time and with the insight of a merciful God who looks not only at the external comforts of life but also the inward growth of the soul. I, for one, am confident when that view can be taken, it will bear out the teachings of the prophets."[3]

I learned another example of this paradox over twenty years later in a conversation with a man who had been excommunicated from the Church. He had committed serious transgressions over a period of time while holding an important Church office in which he counseled Church members. He acknowledged the grievousness of his sins and reported that the Spirit had withdrawn from him in his personal life and in his family responsibilities. At the same time, he stated that the Spirit had continued to help him in a limited way. He had felt its influence to help him function in his Church calling, and he had felt its benefits in the lives of those he led. He said it was significant to him that the Lord would not allow those who came for counsel, trusting in his

2. Letter, September 1978.
3. Letter, September 1978.

calling, to suffer disadvantage because of his sins. That was a new insight for me, and I was grateful to this repentant brother for contributing to my learning by sharing that personal experience.

The Lord sometimes uses even sinful persons to bring good into the lives of His children.

Chapter 38

TESTIMONY OF
JESUS CHRIST

OVER THE COURSE OF MY LIFE I have come to a better understanding of the true significance of a testimony of Christ.

We are followers of Christ and servants of Christ, and we testify of Him. As one of the special witnesses of His name in all the world (D&C 107:23), I testify with the Book of Mormon prophet-king Benjamin that there is "no other name given nor any other way nor means whereby salvation can come unto the children of men, only in and through the name of Christ, the Lord Omnipotent" (Mosiah 3:17).

Jesus Christ is the Only Begotten Son of God the Eternal Father. He is the Creator of this world. Through His incomparable mortal ministry He is our Teacher. Because of His resurrection all who have ever lived will be raised from the dead. He is the Savior whose atoning sacrifice paid for the sin of Adam and opens the door for us to be forgiven of our personal sins so that we can be cleansed to return to the presence of God our Eternal Father. This is the central message of the prophets of all ages. The Prophet Joseph Smith stated this great truth in our third Article of Faith: "We believe that through the Atonement of Christ, all mankind may be saved, by obedience to the laws and ordinances of the Gospel."

I am sometimes asked when and how I acquired my testimony. Like many others raised in the Church, I have difficulty identifying a particular time, event, or experience to answer that question. I have sometimes likened this to such questions as When did you become an adult? or When did you know you loved your wife-to-be? Some important realizations settle upon us gradually, and for me, those include my testimony of Jesus Christ and the truths of the restored gospel.

I can, however, identify experiences that have strengthened my testimony. Some of the most important of these have been acts of service to the Lord and those He loves. That is the principle the Apostle John taught when he wrote, "He that doeth truth cometh to the light" (John 3:21) and "If any man will do his will, he shall know of the doctrine, whether it be of God, or whether I speak of myself" (John 7:17). So it has been in my life. As I have served Him and my fellowmen, I have felt His presence and have come to know Him and the truths of His restored gospel.

That is my testimony of Jesus Christ. But our covenants and our callings require more than the testimony of spoken words. Peter testified, "Thou art the Christ, the Son of the living God," and Jesus called him "Blessed" (Matthew 16:16–17). But much later, Jesus taught this same Peter what he should *do* ("strengthen thy brethren") "when thou art converted" (Luke 22:32). The spoken word of testimony, though blessed, was not enough. There was work to do. In His last teaching to Peter, Jesus commanded, "Feed my sheep" (John 21:16–17), thus reaffirming that the significance of the declared testimony has to be demonstrated by obedient service for Him whom we declare. Many years earlier, King Benjamin gave the same teaching when he challenged his people, "Now, if you believe all these things see that ye do them" (Mosiah 4:10).

When we *know* and when we *testify* to what we know, and when we *do* what we know and testify, then we *become* what God invites us to become. The risen Lord declared, "I would that ye should be perfect even as I, or your Father who is in heaven is perfect" (3 Nephi 12:48). That is the divine invitation for each of us to proceed toward our destiny of eternal life.

The pathway from knowing to testifying to doing and to becoming is long, and there are many distractions. Some distractions can even be created by how we testify. For example, part of the "doing" for a gospel teacher is always to focus his or her teaching on the glory of the Master and the needs of the sheep. Otherwise, with a skillful manner of presenting his or her teachings and testimony, a teacher can become especially popular and find students gathering around him or her. If that is done to "get gain and praise of the world," it is priestcraft (2 Nephi 26:29; see also Alma 1:16). A faithful gospel teacher will never obscure students' view of the Master by standing in the way or by casting a shadow of self-promotion or self-interest.

We should always look to the Master, testify of Him, and do those things that will convert us into what He challenges us to become.

A testimony of Christ should lead us to act on what we know, which will cause us to be converted into what He challenges us to become.

INDEX